N • ERNIE LOMBARDI • WES WESTRUM • BILL TERRY •

WHITEY LOCKMAN • FRANKIE FRISC[...] •

TRAVIS JACKSON • ALVIN DARK • DAV[...] •

[M]ATT WILLIAMS • SID GORDON • JIM DAVENPORT • JIM

[...]E • IRISH MEUSEL • KEVIN MITCHELL • WILLIE MAYS •

[MA]DDOX • MEL OTT • BOBBY BONDS • ROSS YOUNGS •

JUAN MARICHAL • GAYLORD PERRY • SAL MAGLIE •

[ART] NEHF • JOHNNY ANTONELLI • BILLY PIERCE • HOYT

[R]OD BECK • JOHN MCGRAW • LEO DUROCHER • BILL

[M]AHAN • WALKER COOPER • SHANTY HOGAN • ERNIE

[L]OVEY • ORLANDO CEPEDA • JOHNNY MIZE • WHITEY

[...]E • BURGESS WHITEHEAD • EDDIE STANKY • TRAVIS

[...]ELL • BUDDY KERR • FREDDIE LINDSTROM • MATT

[...]ART • BARRY BONDS • MONTE IRVIN • JOE MOORE •

[...]LI DAVIS • HANK LEIBER • BENNY KAUFF • GARRY

[...]N MUELLER • FELIPE ALOU • CHRISTY MATHEWSON

[LA]RRY JANSEN • CARL HUBBELL • RUBE MARQUARD •

[W]ILHELM • STU MILLER • MARV GRISSOM • ROBB NEN

[...] TERRY • DUSTY BAKER • ROGER CRAIG • ROGER

FEW AND CHOSEN

FEW AND CHOSEN

Defining Giants Greatness Across the Eras

Bobby Thomson

with Phil Pepe

TRIUMPH
BOOKS

Library of Congress Cataloging-in-Publication Data

Thomson, Bobby 1923–

    Few and chosen : defining Giants greatness across the eras / Bobby Thomson with Phil Pepe.

      p. cm.

    Includes index.

    ISBN-13: 978-1-57243-854-5

    ISBN-10: 1-57243-854-1

    1. New York Giants (Baseball team)—History. 2. New York Giants (Baseball team)—Biography. 3. Baseball players—United States—Biography. I. Pepe, Phil. II. Title.

GV875.G53T45 2007

796.3570979461—dc22

2006028177

This book is available in quantity at special discounts for your group or organization. For further information, contact:

Triumph Books

542 South Dearborn Street

Suite 750

Chicago, Illinois 60605

(312) 939-3330

Fax (312) 663-3557

Printed in U.S.A.

ISBN: 978-1-57243-854-5

Design by Nick Panos; page production by Patricia Frey

All photos courtesy of AP/Wide World Photos unless indicated otherwise

Contents

Foreword

Ithought I had reached the ultimate pinnacle when the Giants named the body of water right behind right field in SBC Park after me. I'm honored and flattered that they call that little body of water McCovey Cove. Isn't that amazing? Everybody in the Bay Area knows about the Cove.

And I'm just as honored to learn that Bobby Thomson has picked me as the number one first baseman in Giants history. Honored and surprised. I would never have guessed that Bobby would pick me. I'm very flattered by it, especially coming from Bobby, a man I respect a great deal.

I never had the pleasure of playing with Bobby. We missed each other by about a year and a half. I joined the Giants in 1959, and Thomson left them after the 1957 season, but I played against him when he was with the Cubs, and, of course, I have seen him occasionally at Giants alumni events.

I've talked with Bobby, and never once has he mentioned his home run against the Dodgers in the third playoff game in 1951, which many people have called the greatest moment in baseball history. Ballplayers don't usually bring up things like that, and with the kind of man Bobby is, humble and modest, he would certainly never bring it up.

I'm not very close to Bobby, but based on my limited experience with him, I think of him as a gentlemanly guy whom everybody respects. I can't imagine someone like him, with his personality, having any enemies; that's proved by Ralph Branca, who gave up the home run to Bobby. They have become close friends. It shows you the type of man Bobby is, that even Branca ended up liking him.

I was 13 years old in 1951 and living in Mobile, Alabama, where I was born and grew up, and I was a big baseball fan. I was a baseball fan as far back as I could remember. I listened to Game 3 of the 1951 playoff between the Dodgers and Giants. I wanted the Dodgers to win. They were my favorite team because of Jackie Robinson, and they had a minor league team in Mobile. But mainly I was a National League fan. I rooted for Henry Aaron, who also was from Mobile, and I was a big Willie Mays fan. He and Monte Irvin also came from Alabama.

So I wasn't heartbroken when Thomson hit his home run. I was pulling for the Dodgers, but I liked the Giants, too, and I just wanted whoever got into the World Series to beat the Yankees.

I was too young to really appreciate what Thomson did in that game in 1951, but here it is more than 50 years later and nobody has done anything like it. I almost did. In Game 7 of the 1962 World Series, I hit a ball off of Ralph Terry that sailed out of the park foul by just a few inches. Had it stayed fair, it would have won the game—and the Series—and people say they would have elected me mayor of San Francisco.

My ball sailed foul, but Bobby Thomson's didn't. He did it. He came through under great pressure, and you have to respect that. It's something they can never take away from him, and it couldn't have happened to a nicer guy.

—Willie McCovey

Preface

It is said that timing is everything in life. Fate intervenes on all of us and places us in the right (or wrong) place at the right (or wrong) time, and timing, and placement, changes our lives forever.

I am a living example of the truism of both those adages.

What if my father had not decided to leave his native Scotland and had not had the courage to move to the new world, which had to have been a frightening and mysterious adventure for a young man with a large family?

Would I ever have held a baseball bat in my hand or even so much as thrown a baseball?

Would I ever have known the joys and the sorrows, the elation and the frustration I came to experience playing the greatest game ever invented?

Would I ever have known the thrill of playing against Joe DiMaggio and Stan Musial and alongside Willie Mays, Henry Aaron, and Ted Williams, of hitting against Warren Spahn and Sandy Koufax, of playing for Leo Durocher, one of the most colorful, controversial, and complex characters in baseball history?

I suspect, because I was always a pretty good athlete, if I had never come to the United States, I might have been a soccer player. But would I have had the opportunity in soccer, as I did in baseball, to be in the center of what many have called one of the greatest moments in sports?

Right place, right time!

Allow me to dwell on that for a moment.

Suppose the Giants had not put on our second-half rush in the 1951 season, wiped out the Dodgers' 13½ game lead, tied them at the end of the regular season, and forced baseball's first three-game playoff.

What if there had never been a third game, if either team had won the first two?

What if Durocher had not placed me sixth in our batting order, behind Whitey Lockman and in front of Willie Mays?

What if Alvin Dark didn't lead off the bottom of the ninth with a single, or if Gil Hodges did not hold Dark on the base and, as a result, had been able to reach the ground ball by our next hitter, Don Mueller, which also went for a single?

What if the next batter, Monte Irvin, had hit into a double play instead of a foul pop?

What if Lockman didn't follow with a double, putting the tying runs on second and third and knocking Don Newcombe out of the game?

And what if Carl Erskine had not bounced his curveball warming up in the bullpen? If you remember, when Dodgers manager Charlie Dressen asked bullpen coach Clyde Sukeforth which of the two men warming up in the bullpen, Erskine or Ralph Branca, had better stuff, Sukeforth said, "Erskine is bouncing his curveball," and Dressen replied, "Give me Branca."

How would history have changed if Erskine didn't bounce his curveball and he was brought in to pitch to me?

But Erskine did bounce his curveball, and Branca did come in to pitch, and I did hit the home run, the so-called "shot heard 'round the world."

I had a decent major league career (Editor's note: 15 seasons, a .270 lifetime average, 264 home runs, 1,026 RBIs), but if I hadn't been in the right place at the right time in the Polo Grounds, batting against Branca at precisely 3:58 on Wednesday afternoon, October 3, 1951, I would have played my 15 seasons in the major leagues and then vanished from sight and memory, never to be heard from again.

But because I was in the right place at the right time, because of that one at-bat, almost 60 years ago, I'm still remembered. I'm fortunate to have had my one moment in the sun, and I will give myself credit for giving myself a chance to hit. That's why my name still comes up. Without that one moment, I'd have been forgotten long ago. Instead, I still get requests for autographs, still have people tell me they were there in the Polo Grounds that October 3 (the official attendance was 34,320, but I must have had five times that many people tell me they were there), and I still have people who want to talk to me about that home run. And for that I am grateful.

But back to the beginning.

I was born in Glasgow, Scotland, on October 25, 1923, the youngest of six kids. I had four sisters and a brother. Not long after I was born, my dad, James, left Scotland and came to America to settle because he had chosen to raise his children in this country.

Dad was a carpenter, and when you talk about heroes, he was the hero of our family. Imagine a man giving up everything, leaving his home and his family to go halfway around the world because he wanted a better life for his kids and he thought America would give it to us.

Back then, you had to have a sponsor to gain admittance to the United States, and Dad had an old friend from Scotland living on Staten Island, so that's where he headed to find work. After about a year, he had saved enough money to send for his family, and we all set sail for America. I was not quite two and a half at the time, so I don't remember making the trip and I don't remember anything about Scotland. My earliest memories are of living on Staten Island.

Dad had been a soccer player in Scotland, but it wasn't long before he became a big baseball fan. It was probably his way of becoming Americanized.

We didn't have much money, and we didn't even have a car, but I can vividly remember my father taking me to baseball games, which was a special event for a kid who came from a family that had no money. Dad was a Dodgers fan, of all things, my brother was a Yankees fan, but I was always a Giants fan.

I remember going to Ebbets Field with my father to see the Dodgers play the Giants. My dad's favorite player was the Dodgers' first baseman, Dolph Camilli, who was a solid-looking guy with a face that seemed chiseled out of stone. My guy was Mel Ott. I'll never forget, just before the game when the players came on the field, my dad pointed to Ott and said, "There's your man down there."

My dad was a typical Scotsman—ultra-conservative. He preferred to stay in the background. But this day, Camilli hit a home run and I was shocked to see my dad stand up and cheer. I had never seen that kind of reaction from him.

Years later, I met Camilli at an old-timers game on the West Coast and he still looked great. I got a great deal of pleasure telling him that he was my dad's favorite player. I felt good being able to tell him that.

We finally got a family car when I was a teenager and I was getting involved playing baseball all over Staten Island, CYO, PAL, and then at Curtis High School, and Dad always had the car ready to take me to a ballgame. Pretty soon, I began to get a reputation on Staten Island as a baseball player. When I was still in high school, I was asked to play shortstop for a team in an Industrial League with guys who were a few years older than me. One night, there was a Giants scout named George Mack at the game. He had come to look at our center fielder, who had been invited to work out for the Giants a few days later at the Polo Grounds. I had a pretty good game that day, and Mack told our center fielder, "Bring that kid shortstop with you."

I went up to the Polo Grounds and I was in the batter's box taking some swings and I wasn't aware that you had to take five swings and then get out. I'll never forget Dick Bartell telling me, "Get your ass out of there, kid."

The Dodgers were actually more interested in me than the Giants. I had played for the Dodgers Rookies, an amateur team made up of high school kids from the area that the Dodgers wanted to keep their eye on, and I worked out for the Dodgers a few times. The Dodgers asked me not to sign with anybody before talking to them. They said they would better any offer I got from another team.

The Giants offered me $100 a month to go to Bristol, Virginia, in a Class D league. The Dodgers said they would give me $125 a month, but I was a Giants fan and I wanted to play for them.

By this time, I had lost my father, so my brother, Jim, who was nine years older than me, became my mentor. He supported me while I was in high school, and he was the one who talked to the Giants and worked out the details of my contract. The day after I graduated from high school, my brother and I went to New York, downtown to some old building. The contract was on this ledge and I signed the contract on the ledge, and off I went to Bristol, Virginia, nervous and scared and very immature and naïve.

My manager at Bristol was Hal Gruber, and the first day I was there he put me at third base and started hitting ground balls to me. The first ground ball he hit to me hit me on the leg. I was mortified.

Meanwhile, my brother was home wondering how I was doing. Jim played ball himself, a first baseman, but he never got the chance to play professionally. He ended up joining the fire department. So he was at home, and my letters to him were not very encouraging. I was overwhelmed, frustrated, and maybe a little homesick.

Jim had a great deal of common sense, and I got a letter from him, good positive stuff—"don't blame the manager, if you get a chance to get in there, get in there and slide into second, hit somebody, be aggressive," that sort of thing. That was the kind of support Jim gave me. And I'll never forget how he ended the letter: "Your severest critic, but most ardent admirer."

I wasn't doing very well in Bristol, and I wasn't playing much. Bill Terry was the Giants' general manager at the time, and Carl Hubbell was their director of player development. I later heard that one day Terry and Hubbell were talking about me and Hubbell said, "This kid should be playing someplace." Terry agreed, so they moved me to Rocky Mount, North Carolina. I wasn't playing much at Rocky Mount, either, until our third baseman was called into the army and I got a chance to play third.

Before the season ended, I was drafted into the military, and off I went to serve in the U.S. Air Force. While I missed out on the chance to improve my skills in the important early years of minor league baseball, the air force helped me mature. When I got out of the service in 1946, I was invited to spring training in Jacksonville, Florida, with the Giants' Jersey City team of the Triple A International League. The place was overrun with players who had come out of the service.

My sisters were all married, and I was living with my mother and brother on Staten Island. My brother was getting frustrated because there was no news coming out of Jacksonville and he had no way of checking on how I was doing, so one day he took a trip to Jersey City and bought all the Jersey City newspapers. My mother told me that she was working in the yard when my brother came home from Jersey City and she had never seen such a big smile on his face. In one of the Jersey City papers there was a headline about me being "the $100,000 gem" and that I was the ace down there in Jacksonville.

The Giants sent me to Jersey City, their top farm team, to start the 1946 season, and I was in hog heaven. I was playing close to home and the Giants bumped me up to $400 a month. Hey, I was living.

My first game in Jersey City was a historic one, which had nothing to do with me. We played the Montreal Royals, and it happened to be Jackie Robinson's first game in organized baseball. To be honest, I don't remember much about it. I remember getting a couple of hits and that a ball was hit to me that I should have caught, but I couldn't get my legs to move, I was so nervous.

As far as what Jackie did in that game, I don't remember. (Editor's note: Robinson batted second in the lineup for Montreal. His first time up, he grounded weakly to shortstop. Then he rapped out four hits, including a home run, stole two bases, scored twice when he danced off third base and caused the pitcher to balk, and handled every chance at second base flawlessly. The Royals beat the Giants, 14–1.) I just remember he was in all the headlines, and nobody even noticed a scared kid playing center field for the Giants, me.

I was too nervous and scared to understand or appreciate the significance of that game, the first game in which a black man played in organized baseball. I hadn't grown up with any sort of prejudice. In fact, I remember that every Christmas my dad would carry a basket of food over to a black family that apparently didn't have much money. That's just the way I was brought up.

I didn't have a car, and to get from Staten Island to Jersey City I had to take two buses to Bayonne, where I took another bus to Jersey City, and then I'd have to walk about a mile to the ballpark. After a night game, I wouldn't get home until 3:00 in the morning.

That year, they had moved the fences in at Roosevelt Stadium in Jersey City, and I set the team home-run record with 26. I had a good year in Jersey City, and the Giants called me up to New York in September, where I had the pleasure of playing for my baseball hero, Mel Ott. I got in 18 games and batted .315, so when I went to spring training with the Giants in Phoenix in 1947, I thought I had a chance to open the season in center field.

To my surprise, in spring training Ott had me at third base. There were three of us, Sid Gordon, Jack Lohrke, and me, and Ott had us playing third base every third game. One day, Ott was going out to the park early to work on defense with shortstops Buddy Kerr and Bill Rigney and second baseman Buddy Blattner. I was just a young kid all excited about being in spring training with the big club, and I couldn't wait to get out to the park, so I went out with them.

Kerr was working with Blattner and they had me at second base, working with Rigney. I could run, I could move around, I had natural talent. I had never played second base, but Ott was hitting me balls and I was all over the place, getting ground balls. I wasn't aware of what was going on with the team, I was more concerned with how I was doing, but I kept hearing that the Giants might be looking to replace Blattner.

At the time, Cleveland was training in Tucson, so we saw a lot of the Indians, and we teamed up with them for the trip back east. We'd break camp two weeks before the start of the season and take a private train, and we would hedgehop back east, stopping every day to play the Indians in an exhibition game.

One day we were in a tight game with Cleveland and Blattner booted a ball, and instead of going after it he stood rubbing his leg, or something. The Giants were unhappy with Blattner anyway, and that might have been the final straw. After the game, we got back on the train. We were a week out of New York, and I still remember sitting by the side of the tracks when Mel Ott came up to me and said, "How would you like to try second base?"

Second base? I was startled.

Joe Gordon was the Indians' second baseman, and Ott said, "Work with Joe, he'll teach you all you need to know about playing second base."

That's the way it was in those days.

I wound up being the Giants' second baseman on Opening Day. I remember hitting a home run. But my first opportunity for a double play, there was a ball hit to Buddy Kerr at shortstop. I'm playing a little bit of second base and a little bit of right field. I had a tough enough time beating the base runner to the bag much less making a double play. That screwed up the double play.

After about two weeks, I began to get acclimated to playing second and I was enjoying it. I think I could have made it at second base, even though at 6'2" I was tall for a second baseman, but I had enough natural ability and I was a good enough athlete to make it at the position. But we had a bunch of young outfielders and balls were falling in left and right, so Ott came to me again and asked me if I would be willing to play the outfield.

"Of course," I said. "Hey, just let me play."

So Ott put me in left field, but I thought that was a waste because I could really run in those days and I could cover a lot of ground, so I told Ott I thought I was better suited for center field.

"You'd rather play center?" Ott said. "Okay."

He moved me to center and that's where I stayed for the rest of my rookie season.

I was a Giant, a full-fledged major leaguer, but I still didn't have a car, so I would commute from Staten Island to the Polo Grounds by public transportation. I'd have to take a couple of buses to get to the Staten Island Ferry, take the ferry across to New York, and then get on the subway in lower Manhattan and ride all the way up to 155th Street. It took me about two and a half hours to make the trip. But that's how we were brought up in those days. We'd take buses and trains everywhere and thought nothing of it.

I had three sisters living on Staten Island, and occasionally they would come up to the Polo Grounds to see their little brother play. After the game, my sisters and I would get on the subway for the ride home and my sisters, who didn't know left field from right field, would get into a discussion about baseball and start arguing about one thing or another. One of my sisters said, "Here's this little brother of mine playing baseball and making money, I think I'll get my two boys interested in playing baseball." Both her boys turned out to be ministers.

I did pretty well my rookie year, a batting average of .283, 85 runs batted in, and 29 home runs. That was the year we set the major league record for home runs with 221. Johnny Mize hit 51, Willard Marshall 36, Walker Cooper 35, and my 29 was fourth on the team.

I remained an outfielder until May of 1951 when the Giants brought up Willie Mays from Minneapolis to play center field and Durocher moved me back to third base. I hadn't played there in five years, but I took to the position like I had never left, and I had a good year with the bat, an average of .293, 101 runs batted in, and 32 home runs. And I had the good fortune to be in the right place at the right time.

We got off to a terrible start, and the Dodgers were red hot. In July, Dressen made his famous remark, "The Giants is dead," which really got under our skin. We fell behind by 13½ games on August 12, but we weren't dead. We began to play better, and the Dodgers slowed down from their torrid first half. By September 14, we had cut their lead to six games, but we had only 12 games left. Our situation still looked bleak, and even though we won our next five games, we were still four games behind with only seven games left when we went to Boston on September 22 for a three-game series with the Braves.

We won all three games from the Braves, while the Dodgers lost two out of three to the Phillies, and then we won two from the Phillies and the Dodgers lost three out of four in Boston. I kept thinking how strange it was that the guys we had traded away to Boston—Sid Gordon, Walker Cooper, Willard Marshall, and Buddy Kerr—were helping us catch the Dodgers.

We went into the final weekend only a half game behind. We were off on Friday, but we all gathered in a room at the Kenmore Hotel in Boston and listened to the Dodgers game against the Phillies on the radio. The Dodgers lost in Philadelphia and we were tied. I was rooming with Whitey Lockman, and now that we were tied, it suddenly occurred to us that we could lose it. We never did have it, because when you're behind, you're working to get there, and we were never able to catch the Dodgers until now. Whitey and I didn't sleep very much that night, and that had never happened to me before.

We got up the next morning and went down for breakfast, and the lobby of the hotel was jammed. Maybe I'm naïve, but I wasn't expecting the lobby to be crowded. So Whitey and I went into the restaurant for breakfast and we were sitting across from one another. We hadn't said a word up to then, and now we just looked at each other, and we both burst out laughing.

That day we beat the Braves and the Dodgers won in Philadelphia, and it all came down to the final day.

That final game in Boston was the only time I can remember being worried, which is not a good way to play ball. The score was tied and there were runners on base, and who came up to bat but Willard Marshall, one of the players we had traded to the Braves. Normally, you don't think about things like that. You play ball every day, and you just play to the situation. But this time I was worried. I sweated Marshall, who was such a nice guy and a good hitter, and what was going through my mind was, "Wouldn't it be just like him to do it to us." My heart was in my mouth until he hit a fly ball to left field, right at Monte Irvin.

We won our game in Boston and the Dodgers were losing in Philly, and I remember Larry Jansen coming up to me and saying, "Bobby, we're the champs, we're the champs," because the Phillies had a big lead. They had led, 6–2, in the fifth, and then 8–5 in the eighth, and by the time our train got to Grand Central Station, we heard that the Dodgers had won. They had tied the score with three runs in the eighth, and they went to 14 innings. That's when Jackie Robinson had his all-time all-timer, a game-winning home run in the top of the 14th. There was going to be a playoff.

I remember thinking, "Not good, not good." It was very disappointing because we knew the Dodgers were good. We respected their talent, even though they were our rivals and we didn't like them very much. In all the days I played against them, I never talked to any of them except Gil Hodges. Everybody respected Gil.

As the playoffs started, I knew we were getting into pennant stuff, and the thought in my mind was, "How are you going to handle it, buddy boy? How are you going to conduct yourself? Are you going to go out there and play ball like a pro? Like a big leaguer? How are you going to perform under pressure?"

The first time I checked myself was when Carl Furillo, leading off an inning, topped a ball down the third-base line where you have to go in and field the ball with your bare hand and throw on the run. I handled that, threw him out, and I said to myself, "Hey, okay, kid. That wasn't bad. You're going to be all right."

We won that first game in Ebbets Field, a tight game, 3–1, and then in the second game in the Polo Grounds we got killed, 10–0. That hurt. I was the last guy to leave the locker room. I went out with some friends from Staten Island and had a few drinks and just relaxed, and then I went home and got a good night's sleep.

You never know how you're going to react in a situation like this, and driving up to the Polo Grounds the next day—I had a car by then—I remember thinking, "If you get three hits today, it should help us win this ballgame." I never had thoughts like that before.

I got to the park and I could feel the tension in the air. I got dressed and went out onto the field to warm up. I was throwing the ball around, getting loose, and I looked around and there was Al Dark, our captain and a very competitive guy, a real pro, and I'm thinking, "I'm glad Al's on our team. Monte Irvin. I'm glad he's on our team." I had never done that before. Why was I doing it then? Was I looking for help? For comfort? I can't explain it.

That's how the game started, and there was the usual tenseness, and I screwed up a play early in the game that cost us. Lockman was on first base, and I hit a ball that I felt was a certain double down the left-field line. I figured I could get out of the box and be standing on second easily and Whitey, who could run, would get to third base, at least, so I started running, head down, and never realized Whitey, for some reason, had stopped at second. When I looked up, there we were, both standing on second base. I got in a rundown and tried to avoid the tag, but I was out, and a potential big inning was snuffed out. That's not very good. So I was wrong.

In my mind, I was thinking you've got to do something. Normally, that would have bothered me. When you screw up, you're thinking about yourself. You're not even aware of the fans. This was a different situation. I was never in a situation like that. All I was thinking about was winning. I forgot about the mistake I made.

We didn't score that inning and the game was a nail-biter. The Dodgers had scored a run in the first, and it was still 1–0 in the seventh inning. Irvin hit a double, and Lockman bunted him over to third. I came to bat, the toughest at-bat I ever had. I was fighting for my life. I felt like Don Newcombe, their starting pitcher, was throwing the ball 135 miles an hour.

I was swinging at everything, outside, inside. I took a ball and the next pitch Newcombe came outside again and I just reached out, stuck my bat out, and hit a pretty good fly ball to Duke Snider in center field. Monte scored from third, and we were tied, 1–1.

But the Dodgers scored three runs in the eighth, and you could feel the air coming out of our balloon, and I was the culprit once again. They had a run in and runners on first and third when Andy Pafko hit a slow bouncing ball down the third-base line, a do-or-die play, an in-between hop. It hit my glove, but I didn't come up with it. I didn't get an error, but I should have made the play. That brought in the second run.

Hodges popped up, but Billy Cox hit a shot to third, the only ball like that I had ever seen. It hit the grass and just skipped in front of me. I never got my glove up and it got by me. Another run was in and we were down, 4–1, with only three outs left. I can't remember ever feeling lower in my career. When the inning was over, I went to the dugout and threw my glove down onto the dugout floor in disgust. I was thinking we just weren't good enough to take that last step. The Dodgers were too tough, and I was the goat. I wasn't even thinking about redemption. It was just total dejection.

Then, before you knew it, a little ground ball by Dark went through the infield. Another ground ball by Don Mueller, not hit hard, but past Hodges, who was holding the runner on base with a three-run lead when he should have been playing off the bag to cut off a hit. Now two guys were on base and Monte Irvin, our big guy, the guy responsible more than anybody for getting us there, was at bat. But I guess it just wasn't Monte's time. He hit a foul pop.

Lockman was next and he hit a line drive double to left field, the first decently hit ball in the inning. Second and third, and I was in the on-deck circle, getting ready to get up to the plate. I looked up and saw Mueller lying on the ground. I never even saw him slide. As soon as Whitey hit the ball, I headed for the plate and there's poor Mueller on the ground. It wasn't until they carried him off the field that I realized he had injured his ankle. The delay kind of broke the tension for a moment, but once Mueller was taken off the field I thought, "Back to baseball."

The next thing I remember was Leo Durocher, coming down from the third-base coach's box and putting his arm around my shoulder and saying, "Bobby, if you ever hit one, hit one now," and I thought, "He's never put his arm around me before."

I didn't pay any attention to him. I thought, "You're out of your mind." Nobody goes up to bat trying to hit a home run in a situation like that. If you do, you're almost certain to fail. I was just hoping to make contact.

People have asked me, "What was it like? What was the crowd like?"

My answer is, "What crowd?" I was alone in the world.

Recently, I got a call from Larry Bowa. It was after he had been fired as manager of the Phillies and before he became a coach with the Yankees and he was doing some radio work. He called me to talk about the home run, and the first words out of his mouth were, "What was your mindset when you went up to bat?"

An interesting question. What was my mindset? That's what it's all about. Mindset. Walking to the plate, I did something I had never done before. I was talking to myself. I was thinking four things. "Get up there and do a good job. Wait and watch. Don't get overanxious. Give yourself a chance to hit." And I was calling myself a son of a bitch. I was doing that to get determined, aggressive. I reminded myself not to make too fast a move, to sit back, wait, and watch.

When I got to home plate, I looked out, and there was Ralph Branca on the mound. They had changed pitchers. I hadn't even noticed it; so much was going on—Mueller being carried off the field and the Dodgers changing pitchers—and I never noticed any of it. I was in another world, alone with my thoughts.

I got up to bat, and I had a mindset I had never had before. If I had had that mindset more often, like Stan Musial, total concentration, I would be in the Hall of Fame. I had enough natural ability to do better in my career than I did, but I was inconsistent, one good year, one bad year. That's not good. And you wonder why. What's the reason? Didn't I try hard enough?

Al Dark was as competitive a guy as I ever played with and, apparently, I wasn't that competitive. But I was when it counted, during the playoffs, in terms of my attitude and not thinking about myself.

I was in the batter's box, and the first pitch from Branca was right through the middle. I took it, and the guys told me later they wanted to kill me for taking that pitch.

All I remember about the next pitch is that it was high and inside, and I just got a glimpse of it. I remember thinking later that I was lucky to hit that thing. Branca was satisfied he had made a good pitch, but I was quick with my hands and it wasn't bad enough that I couldn't get around on it.

And then all the excitement, people going crazy, Eddie Stanky running out of the dugout to the third-base coach's box and jumping on Durocher, and I was running around the bases and being mobbed by my teammates at home plate, getting pounded on the back, and being swallowed up in a sea of humanity. I had never experienced anything like that before.

When I got home to Staten Island that night, I told my brother Jim, my mentor, "Jim, don't ask me what happened up there today. The Good Lord had to have something to do with it."

Jim said, "No, Bob, no, Bob, do you realize what you did?"

"Of course, Jim, I was there."

"No," he said. "Something like that may never happen again."

I never thought about it that way. To me, all it meant was that we beat our archrivals, the Dodgers. Obviously, the home run changed my life, but not as much as you might think. I certainly didn't get rich off it.

After the season, I had an offer to go to New England, a few stops to make a few appearances, and I would be paid $800. I turned it down.

I had one endorsement before the home run. In those days, the endorsements went to the big guys, Joe DiMaggio and Ted Williams. The Yankees were the big guys in New York: DiMaggio, Phil Rizzuto, Yogi Berra. They got most of the endorsements. The Giants were second-class citizens in town. But then, Sal Maglie and Larry Jansen started to get a name, and they got some endorsements, and I started thinking, "What about me?"

I had had a good year in 1949 (.309, 109 RBIs, 27 home runs), and I got an endorsement from a tobacco company for about $1,000. Then I had a bad year in 1950 (.252, 85, 25) and they said, "Sorry, we can't use you."

So I didn't have any endorsements in 1951, but after I hit the home run, the tobacco company called me and wanted to renew my contract. I told them I wanted the same contract that DiMaggio and Williams had. I could have made it tough on them. I could have held them up for more, but that wasn't my style. And I didn't have an agent. So I took what they offered, about $2,000 or $3,000, which was pretty good money in those days—about 10 percent of my playing salary. And that was it. That's all the extra money I made off that home run, outside of my playing contract.

The Giants paid me $23,000 in 1951 and they offered me a $2,000 raise. I didn't sign. That winter, I was in Boston with Durocher at a banquet. We were sitting next to each other on the dais and Leo said to me, "What are you asking?" I said, "$15,000." And Durocher patted me on the knee and said, "You're okay."

Durocher might have known something, or maybe he took that information back to the owner, Horace Stoneham, because the next day, I went home by train and the Giants called me and said, "Come on up and sign your contract." I got my $15,000 raise.

After the home run, I would spend two more years with the Giants, until I was traded to the Braves in 1954.

Times were different then. I had to work in the off-season, and when I retired, I was married and had a child, and there were no offers for jobs in baseball, as a coach or a scout, so I had to go out and get a job. I had a good friend, a lawyer, who suggested different companies in various fields and arranged job interviews for me.

One day, I was leaving New York, going to Grand Central Station to take the train to Staten Island. As I was crossing the street, some man came up behind me and told me he was a Giants fan and he recognized my walk. He happened to be the president of Canada Dry, and I told him I was looking for work, so he invited me to come in for an interview.

I had another interview with American Cyanamid. That interview was with Gen. Anthony Clement McAuliffe, who gained fame during the Battle of the Bulge in World War II. He was commanding the 101st Airborne Division at Bastogne, Belgium, when he received a surrender ultimatum from the Germans. Gen. McAuliffe's famous reply was one word, "Nuts."

I ended up taking a job on Park Avenue in New York City in sales with West Virginia Pulp & Paper, a company that planted seedlings to develop their own timberlands, and out of that they made paper. I commuted to New York from Staten Island every day. I'd have to take two trains to get there and two trains back. I did that for years.

That's how it was back then, before unions and agents and free agency. But I have no regrets. Now, more than 60 years after the home run, as I look back, I'm happy to have had an opportunity like that, to have had my one moment. How many guys have had an opportunity like that?

I consider myself fortunate to have played during baseball's golden era in New York City, with three teams—the Yankees in the Bronx, the Giants in Manhattan, and the Dodgers in Brooklyn—each of them a contender. In fact, in the seven years I was a Giant, there was a New York team in the World Series every year except one, and it was an all–New York World Series in five of those years.

I played in a magical and simpler time—before expansion, free agency, interleague play, and the designated hitter. And I played with, and against, some of the greatest players the game has known—Joe DiMaggio, Mickey Mantle, Yogi Berra, Whitey Ford, Jackie Robinson, Roy Campanella, Duke Snider, Willie Mays, Ted Williams, Stan Musial, Henry Aaron, Frank Robinson, Warren Spahn, Robin Roberts…I could go on and on.

I admit to a certain prejudice regarding the players of my day, and if it seems that in my selections for my all-Giants team I have favored those of my era, I offer no defense and no apologies.

The Giants have had many great players, more Hall of Famers than any other team, many of them before my time. I don't feel qualified to judge those I never saw play, although some, like Christy Mathewson, Frank Frisch, Bill Terry, and Carl Hubbell, I know from the observation of others and, from looking at their records, are no-brainers.

I apologize if I have offended anyone, but I make no claim that my team is official; it's merely one man's opinion.

—Bobby Thomson

Acknowledgments

This book is dedicated to the hundreds of men who proudly wore the black and orange of the Giants on two coasts, and to those who served the Giants just as proudly without ever putting on a uniform.

The authors also wish to acknowledge and thank those who so willingly, graciously, and generously gave of their time to talk about Giants of the past: Ralph Kiner, Bobby Cox, Alvin Dark, Monte Irvin, Larry Jansen, Phil Niekro, Keith Hernandez, Rusty Staub, Ron Darling, and Hall of Fame baseball writer Jack Lang. They were not all Giants, but they are all giants.

Introduction

No team in all of baseball has a longer, or more storied, history than the Giants of New York and San Francisco, comprising a century and a quarter of uninterrupted baseball excellence (mostly) on two coasts and featuring some of the greatest games and names in baseball lore.

Fifty-two men who wore the Giants uniform are enshrined in the Baseball Hall of Fame in Cooperstown, New York, more than any other team. And while some like Rogers Hornsby, Burleigh Grimes, Waite Hoyt, Gabby Hartnett, Tony Lazzeri, Joe Medwick, Joe Morgan, Hack Wilson, Duke Snider, Red Schoendienst, Warren Spahn, Steve Carlton, and Gary Carter made only cameo appearances, others like Roger Bresnahan, Buck Ewing, Christy Mathewson, Frankie Frisch, Carl Hubbell, Mel Ott, Freddie Lindstrom, Juan Marichal, John McGraw, Willie McCovey, and Willie Mays were giants of the game, and Giants through and through.

- A Giant, pitcher Mickey Welch, was the first pinch-hitter in major league history on September 10, 1889. He struck out.
- A Giant, Arlie Latham, was the first full-time coach put under contract, in 1907.
- A Giant, Roger Bresnahan, was the first catcher to wear shin guards, on April 11, 1907.
- It was while passing the Polo Grounds, where the Giants played their games, that composer Jack Norworth, who had never seen a major

league game, got the inspiration to write the song, "Take Me Out to the Ball Game," in 1908.

- A Giant, Bill Terry, was the last National Leaguer to bat over .400 (.401 in 1930).
- At the time he retired in 1947, a Giant, Mel Ott, had hit more home runs (511) than any other National League player.

The Giants, replacing a team from Troy in upstate New York, entered the National League in 1883 as the New York Gothams or Green Stockings, under the ownership of John B. Day, a tobacco merchant, and Jim Mutrie, a sports entrepreneur. At the same time, Day and Mutrie entered another New York team, the Metropolitans, in the American Association.

The Gothams played their first game on May 1, 1883, on a tract of land from 110th to 112th Streets between Fifth and Sixth Avenues in upper Manhattan that had once been used for polo, and thus was called the Polo Grounds. In their National League debut, the Gothams defeated Boston, 7–5, before a crowd estimated at 15,000 that included former President Ulysses S. Grant.

When the original Polo Grounds burned to the ground in 1911, the Giants moved further uptown, to 155th Street adjacent to the Harlem River, and took the name Polo Grounds with them.

In order to protect his investment, Mutrie managed the Metropolitans himself and won the American Association pennant in 1884, while the Gothams, under Jim Price and then Monte Ward, finished fifth in the eight-team National League. Flushed with his success, Mutrie switched over to manage the Gothams in 1885, taking several members of his champion Mets with him. Under Mutrie, the Gothams moved up to second place, so he stayed on as manager for six more years, winning National League pennants in 1888 and '89.

Mutrie was a bear of a man, resplendent in frock coat, stovepipe hat, and cane and sporting a flowing handlebar mustache. He was proud of his Gothams, many of whom stood 6' in height and taller, considered gigantic at the time. Mutrie would parade around referring to his players as, "My boys, my giants."

Newspapers jumped on the name and began referring to the New York National League team as the Giants, and Giants they have remained.

After their initial success under Day and Mutrie, the Giants fell on hard times in the last decade of the 19th century. By 1900, they had plummeted into the basement of the National League. To remedy the situation, the Giants spirited the bombastic and pugnacious John McGraw away from the Baltimore club with a four-year contract at $11,000 per year, a king's ransom at the time, and made him their manager.

Under McGraw's progressive and fiery leadership, the Giants became the most successful team in baseball, both on the field and at the turnstiles, over the first quarter of the 20th century. McGraw remained leader of the Giants for 31 seasons, during which he won 10 pennants, finished second 11 times, and third four times, a record unmatched by any other team at the time.

When McGraw shocked the baseball world by resigning as manager a quarter of the way through the 1932 season, he was replaced by first baseman Bill Terry, who guided the Giants to three more pennants in 10 years, the last in 1937.

The Giants would wait 14 years before winning another National League pennant under Leo Durocher in 1951 when they staged the greatest comeback in baseball history. Trailing the first place Dodgers by 13½ games on August 12, the Giants stormed back to end the regular season tied with the Dodgers and then won the National League's second three-game playoff, two games to one.

Three years later, led by the fabulous Willie Mays, who won the league batting championship with a .345 average, hit 41 home runs, and drove in 110 runs, the Giants won another pennant under Durocher and swept the Cleveland Indians in the World Series, four games to none.

Over the next three years, the Giants again fell on hard times. In 1956 they finished in sixth place, and attendance had fallen from a high of 1,600,793 in 1947 to a mere 629,179.

When Dodgers owner Walter O'Malley decided to pick up stakes and move from Brooklyn to Los Angeles, he persuaded Giants owner Horace Stoneham to join in and resume their rivalry on the country's West Coast. In 1958, the Giants moved to San Francisco, taking their history, their tradition, and their star, Willie Mays, with them. For the first two years in San Francisco, the Giants played in Seals Stadium, which had been the home of a Pacific Coast League team, while their own ballpark was being constructed.

Candlestick Park opened in 1960 and remained the home of the Giants for 40 seasons, until a brand-new stadium was opened in 2000.

Along the way, the Giants were involved in some of the greatest games and most spectacular moments in baseball history and were at the center of some of the game's most memorable quotes.

- "Is Brooklyn still in the league?" asked Giants manager Bill Terry in 1934 after the Giants had won the 1933 pennant and the Dodgers had finished sixth. The remark came back to haunt Terry when the Dodgers beat the Giants in the final two games of the 1934 season and knocked them out of a second straight pennant.
- "Nice guys finish last." The quote, attributed to Leo Durocher, found its way into Bartlett's "Famous Quotations." Its origin was late in the 1946 season when Durocher's Dodgers were battling the Cardinals for first place, while the Giants, managed by Mel Ott, languished in last place.

  Talking with Brooklyn announcer Red Barber before a game between the Dodgers and Giants, and pointing to his counterpart Mel Ott across the field, what Durocher actually said was, "Look over there. Do you know a nicer guy than Mel Ott? Or any of the other Giants? Why, they're the nicest guys in the world. And where are they? In last place."

  Two years later, Durocher would replace Ott as manager of the Giants.
- "The Giants is dead." The inflammatory, if ungrammatical, remark was made by Dodgers manager Charlie Dressen in July of 1951, with the Dodgers seemingly running away with the National League pennant and the Giants struggling to get out of the second division. The Giants, under Durocher, would come back to catch the Dodgers and beat them in a playoff.

And there were memorable moments in Giants history:

- Matty's Mastery: The legendary Christy Mathewson, who would win 373 games, performed the unmatched feat of pitching three shutouts in a six-day span against the Philadelphia Athletics in the 1905 World Series.

- Merkle's Boner: On September 23, 1908, Giants first baseman Fred Merkle was on first base when Al Bridwell hit an apparent game-winning single in the bottom of the ninth against the Cubs. While Moose McCormick scored from third with what was believed to be the winning run, Merkle, instead of touching second base, turned and headed for the dugout, as was the custom of the day. Cubs second baseman Johnny Evers called for the ball and stepped on second base, claiming the force-out negated the winning run.

   Umpires ruled in the Cubs' favor and the game remained tied, but because the crowd had stormed the playing field in celebration, the game could not be resumed. It would be made up, if needed, after the final game of the season.

   When the Giants and Cubs finished the season tied for first place, the game was replayed. The Cubs won the make-up game and the National League pennant.
- Homer Haven: Playing in the cozy Polo Grounds, with its short left field and right field walls, the Giants set a major league record by bashing 221 home runs in 1947.
- Willie's Catch: With the Giants and Indians tied, 2–2, and two runners on base in the eighth inning of Game 1 of the 1954 World Series, with his back to home plate, Willie Mays made a spectacular, over-the-shoulder catch of Vic Wertz's drive to right-center field, 460 feet away. The catch preserved the tie, which the Giants broke on Dusty Rhodes's three-run, pinch-hit home run in the bottom of the 10th, and went on to sweep the Series in four games.

   Mays has often said that the catch was not the best one he ever made, but because of the situation, the timing, and the World Series atmosphere, it was his most memorable, and the signature catch of his legendary career.
- Barry's Blasts: In 2001, Barry Bonds obliterated the major league single-season home-run record by blasting 73 out of the park, many of them into McCovey Cove, a body of water beyond the right-field fence in SBC Park.

- The shot heard 'round the world: By most accounts, it's the greatest single moment in baseball history—Bobby Thomson's three-run home run in the bottom of the ninth of the third game of the 1951 playoff against the Dodgers. It came with two on, one out, and the Dodgers leading, 4–2.

There has been no bigger story in baseball, ever, no single moment that has had such an impact at the time and through the ages. It still resonates almost 60 years later. And there has been no sports idol as unassuming and selfless as the man who struck that historic blow.

Accordingly, there is no one better qualified to select an all-time Giants team, the top five players at each position, plus the five greatest Giants managers.

Thomson's association with the Giants dates back almost 70 years, to 1942, when as an 18-year-old just out of high school, he signed his first professional contract with the Giants. He hasn't seen all the great Giants in history, but suffice it to say that in those more than six decades he has seen most of them.

—Phil Pepe

ONE

Catcher

To be honest, I can't tell you much about **Roger Bresnahan**. I have no idea how good a catcher he was. What I can tell you is that you can't be around baseball for any length of time without having heard the name Roger Bresnahan. He was the first Giants non-pitcher elected to the Hall of Fame, and, in fact, he and Ernie Lombardi are the *only* Giants catchers in the Hall of Fame.

That alone is reason enough to rate Bresnahan as number one on the all-time list of Giants catchers. But there's more.

Bresnahan actually played all over the lot, in the outfield, all four infield positions, and he even pitched in nine games, but catcher was his primary position in his 17-year career.

What made Bresnahan a household name in his day—the early days of baseball, just after the turn of the 20th century—is that he was a mainstay on a Giants team that won two National League championships in his six and a half years, and he was the favorite catcher of the great Christy Mathewson. It was Bresnahan who was behind the plate when Matty pitched three shutouts against the Philadelphia Athletics in the 1905 World Series.

1. ROGER BRESNAHAN

2. WALKER COOPER

3. SHANTY HOGAN

4. ERNIE LOMBARDI

5. WES WESTRUM

2

Roger Bresnahan is credited with inventing the catcher's shin pads, which he supposedly modeled after the equipment that was used in cricket. *Photo courtesy MLB Photos via Getty Images.*

To add to the Bresnahan lore, he is credited with inventing the catcher's shin guards, which he modeled after the leg pads worn by cricket players.

Bresnahan started his career in 1897 as an 18-year-old pitcher with the Washington Senators, then in the National League. When he held out for more money after winning four games and losing none, the Senators let him go and the Cubs picked him up. In 1901, Bresnahan became a free agent and was signed by John McGraw for the Baltimore Orioles, beginning a long relationship between the two men.

McGraw and Bresnahan were kindred spirits, both temperamental, pugnacious, Irish brawlers who were tough on umpires, opponents, and teammates alike, and they became close friends. Bresnahan was constantly in trouble. He was frequently ejected from games, suspended, and fined, and he often engaged in confrontations with team owners; in short, he was McGraw's kind of player.

McGraw and Bresnahan were kindred spirits, both temperamental, pugnacious, Irish brawlers who were tough on umpires, opponents, and teammates alike.

When McGraw was hired away from Baltimore to manage the Giants in 1902, he brought his pal Bresnahan with him. The Giants already had two catchers in place, so McGraw put Bresnahan in center field. Legend has it that Mathewson urged McGraw to make Bresnahan his catcher and a Hall of Fame career was launched.

After the 1908 season, the St. Louis Cardinals, hoping to add some of McGraw's fire to their perennial cellar-dwelling team, traded three of their best players to the Giants for Bresnahan and made him their player/manager.

Bresnahan showed the Cardinals fire, all right, but it was directed at the team's owner. As a manager, Bresnahan was a failure. His Cardinals finished seventh, seventh, fifth, and sixth in his four years and he was let go after the 1912 season and sold to the Cubs, where he was a back-up catcher for two seasons before taking over as their manager in 1915. He played one more season and then retired.

In later years, Bresnahan was owner-manager of the minor league Toledo Mud Hens, his hometown team, and a coach for the Giants under his pal McGraw, and of the Tigers. He was elected to the Hall of Fame in 1945, the year after he died, and, coincidentally, the year before I joined the Giants.

Walker Cooper hit the ball harder than anybody I ever played with, and I played with Johnny Mize, Willie Mays, and Henry Aaron. If you want to compare him to today's players, as far as how hard he hit the ball, the closest would be Gary Sheffield.

Coop had been an outstanding catcher for the Cardinals, teaming with his brother, Mort, to form probably the best brother battery in baseball history and helping the Cards win three consecutive pennants, from 1942 to 1944. Then he went off to the navy, and the Giants bought him while he was still in service. They paid $175,000 for him— a lot of money in those days.

The Cooper brothers were a couple of cowboys from Missouri, country boys. They'd come into New York with the Cardinals by train and they'd laughed at the hot-shot New York city slickers. They loved to play games on the train. They'd put something on the floor of the train, like a bow tie or something, that was attached to a string in their pocket and when somebody would go to pick up the bow tie, Mort or Walker would pull the string and yank it away. Silly stuff like that.

Coop told me that in the hotel lobby, he'd put a newspaper on the floor in front of where he was sitting and one of those New York city slickers would go to pick up the paper and Coop would look at the guy and say, "That's not your paper," so the guy would slink off all embarrassed.

The 1946 season was only a few days old when Cooper broke his finger and was sidelined for quite a while. When that injury healed, he suffered other ailments that left him with only 280 at-bats, eight home runs, 46 runs batted in, and a .268 average. The next year, the Giants got the Walker Cooper they thought they were getting for their $175,000. Coop had the best season of his career.

That was the year the Giants set the National League record with 221 home runs. We had four of the league's top five home-run hitters—Mize, who tied Ralph Kiner for the league lead with 51; Willard Marshall, third with 36; Cooper, fourth with 35; and I was fifth with 29. Coop was third in the league, behind Mize and Kiner, in runs batted in with 122. And Coop batted .305.

Hal Schumacher, who won 158 games for the Giants in the 1930s and 1940s, had retired after the 1946 season and went to work for the Dolgeville Bat Company, the makers of Adirondack bats. Because he was an old Giant, he provided us with bats and, as a favor to Hal, the guys used his bats, so we

Walker Cooper (second from left) was not only a great catcher but also one of the hardest-hitting players in the history of the game. He is shown with, from left, Willard Marshall, Whitey Lockman, and Johnny Mize.

were the first ones to use Adirondack bats. We felt those bats had the best wood we had ever used. Whether it was true or not, I don't know, but when we set the all-time home-run record, that really helped put Adirondack on the map.

Watching Cooper hit with the Adirondack, I used to think there was iron in those bats. In fact, there was. Cooper used to hammer nails into his bats, until the other teams noticed the nails and the umpires made him stop.

But Coop didn't need nails to hit the ball hard. He wasn't a guy like Joe DiMaggio, who kept both feet planted. He'd step with his front foot and he'd tomahawk balls and he hit the hardest balls I've seen hit. He was a tough guy. He had an unusual way of hitting. He would cock the bat before he swung, dropping it so that the bat was parallel to the ground, and then he would bring it back and whip it and hit the ball hard…boom…boom…boom, like Sheffield. You have to be strong to do that, and Coop, who was 6'3" and about 220 pounds, was strong. Ewell Blackwell said Cooper was the strongest man he's ever known.

Despite setting the National League record for home runs, the Giants finished in fourth place in 1947, and so when Leo Durocher took over midway in the 1948 season, he began to get rid of all those slow-footed sluggers and replaced them with younger, faster players and put more of an emphasis on speed, defense, and pitching. Cooper was one of the first to go when he was traded to Cincinnati midway through the 1949 season, and Durocher made Wes Westrum his catcher.

Durocher and Cooper never formed a mutual admiration society in the first place. I heard that when he was in St. Louis, Coop and his brother would tie a string to a watch and dangle it so that Leo could see it. That was because of the famous story that when Leo was a young player with the Yankees, he went into the players' valuables box and stole Babe Ruth's watch, a story that never was proved and that Durocher always denied.

Later Coop went on to play for the Braves, the Pirates, and the Cubs, and then he finished up his career where he started, in St. Louis. Coop always could hit. He had some good years after he left the Giants, batting over .300 in 1950, 1951, and 1954, and finishing with a career average of .285 for 18 seasons. But he never again came close to his 1947 numbers in home runs and RBIs.

Cooper was with the Giants only three and a half seasons, but he certainly made his mark in that short time and left a lasting impression on me.

Like Roger Bresnahan, Shanty (his real name was James Francis, but he was called "Shanty" because, at 6"1', and 240 pounds, he was built like a house) Hogan is someone I know little about, but who I heard about from old timers when I was a Giant.

A check of his record told me that **Shanty Hogan** was a career .295 hitter for 13 seasons, and that after he was traded to the Giants in 1928 by the Boston Braves in a deal for Rogers Hornsby, he batted over .300 for four straight seasons.

Hogan had the reputation of being a consistent, high average hitter and a durable and excellent defensive catcher who once played 120 consecutive errorless games behind the plate, 18 short of the National League record for catchers.

Hogan spent five years with the Giants for whom he had career highs in batting average (.339 in 1930), home runs (13 in 1930), and RBIs (77 in 1932). After his time with the Giants, Hogan returned to the Braves, and then finished out his career with the Washington Senators.

I'm putting **Ernie Lombardi** fourth on my list of all-time Giants catchers, even though he was a Giant for only five seasons and at the end of his career.

Lombardi came to the Giants during World War II, when so many players were in military service. He was mostly a back-up catcher by then, but he still batted over .300 twice and over .280 four times in five seasons.

I was Lombardi's teammate briefly, in 1946 and 1947. They called him "Schnozz" because of his prominent nose. He was at the end of his career, almost 40 years old, and he got in only 136 games, mostly as a pinch-hitter.

Schnozz didn't say much, he'd just sit on the bench with his catcher's mitt under his arm like a pancake, and when manager Mel Ott needed a pinch-hitter, he'd walk down the bench to where Schnozz was sitting and point to him. The first thing Lombardi would do was put down his glove and slowly tie his shoes, first one, and then the other. Then he'd walk over and grab a bat out of the bat rack, this big, heavy piece of lumber, and amble up to the plate, dragging his bat along the ground. He'd never take a practice swing. He'd just get in the batter's box and get ready to hit. And he could hit, even at the end of his career.

He batted .290 and .282 in his last two years and hit 16 homers in 348 at-bats.

Ernie Lombardi was a career .306 hitter as well as a great defensive catcher with a rifle for an arm. *Photo courtesy of MLB Photos via Getty Images.*

To me, Schnozz was an old guy, and very quiet. He wouldn't say much, but he'd walk around the locker room singing "Mairzy Doats and Doezy Doats," a novelty song that was very popular at the time. Lombardi loved that song. He'd go around singing it all the time. He was quite a character.

I said earlier that Walker Cooper hit the ball harder than anybody I've seen, but I didn't see enough of Lombardi at his peak. From what I heard, he might have hit the ball as hard as Coop. The little I saw of Schnozz at the end of his career was enough to convince me how great a hitter he must have been in his prime.

The man could hit. He had an unusual way of hitting, with his fingers interlocked so he could get a better grip on the bat, which was the heaviest in the league. And he hit the ball hard. But he couldn't run. He hit the ball so hard, and ran so slow, that infielders would play him on the outfield grass and still be able to throw him out. One night, against the Dodgers, Lombardi figured he'd cross up the defense. He dropped down a bunt and lumbered to first base. The infield was so deep, Ernie was able to beat it out for a hit. It was such a shock that the headline in one New York newspaper the next day was: "Lombardi Beats Out Bunt."

Ernie Lombardi hit the ball so hard, and ran so slow, that infielders would play him on the outfield grass and still be able to throw him out.

In his prime, he was one of the best hitters in the National League and an outstanding catcher with a great arm. He was the catcher for both of Johnny Vander Meer's consecutive no-hitters in 1938 and was a mainstay on the Cincinnati team that won back-to-back pennants in 1939 and 1940.

His lifetime batting average of .306 for 17 seasons included two batting titles. In 1938, he led the league with a .342 average, only the second catcher to win a batting championship (Bubbles Hargrave, also of the Reds, had won it 12 years before) and was named National League Most Valuable Player. Four years later, Lombardi won a second batting title with a .330 average for the Braves, making him the only catcher to win two batting championships. Not bad for a guy who couldn't run.

After he retired, Lombardi became a fixture at Candlestick Park, working as a press box and press room attendant. He was a likable guy, but he never hid his disappointment at being bypassed in the Hall of Fame voting.

Lombardi finally was elected to the Hall of Fame in 1977 by the Veterans Committee. Sadly, it came almost nine years after his death.

9

$\mathcal{F}$or more than six decades, Jack Lang has been affiliated with major league baseball, as the longtime secretary-treasurer of the Baseball Writers Association of America and as beat writer for the Long Island (New York) Press of first the Brooklyn Dodgers and, from their inception, the New York Mets for the Press, and later the New York Daily News.

Lang has known Wes Westrum as a player, a coach, and a manager, traveling with the Mets during Westrum's four-year tenure as a coach and manager.

"Leo Durocher loved him as a player," Lang recalled. "Westrum was an exceptional defensive catcher with occasional home-run power, but what Leo loved about him most was his defensive ability, the way he called a game and the way he handled that great Giants pitching staff in the 1950s of [Sal] Maglie, [Larry] Jansen, [Jim] Hearn, and [Dave] Koslo."

Lang remembers attending the 1963 All-Star Game in Cleveland and one night sharing a cab with Casey Stengel in search of a local watering hole:

> We're driving through midtown and Stengel spots a red sign on a bar and says, "There's one that's still open, let's go."
>
> Casey tells the cabbie to stop and we got out and went into the bar and ordered a drink. I looked up and noticed a guy sitting all alone in the back, sipping a beer. It was Westrum, who was a coach for the San Francisco Giants at the time. I knew him from his playing days with the Giants, but Casey had never met him. I walked to the back of the bar and invited Westrum to join us, and he did. After awhile, I decided to go back to my hotel because it was getting late and I left Westrum and Stengel at the bar, talking baseball.
>
> That winter, the Mets announced that they had traded coaches with the Giants. Cookie Lavagetto, who had been a Mets coach, wanted to go back to northern California, so George Weiss [the Mets general manager] arranged a deal with the Giants. They would take Lavagetto as a coach and, in exchange, the Mets would take Westrum to be their first-base coach. I have no doubt that it came out of that night Stengel met Westrum for the first time and spent time talking baseball with him.

According to Lang, Westrum had earned a reputation for his ability to pick up pitches. "Willie Mays often said that Westrum tipped him off to a lot of pitches during his career," said Lang.

Westrum joined the Mets in the spring of 1964 as first-base coach under Stengel. Midway through the 1965 season, Stengel fell and broke his hip. From his hospital bed, Stengel told Weiss to let Westrum manage the team for the remainder of the season.

Said Lang:

> We were all surprised that Casey chose Westrum. We thought he'd pick Yogi Berra, who had come over to the Mets from the Yankees that year, tried to play, but when he got only two hits in nine at-bats, Yogi decided to retire and the Mets made him a coach. Casey always referred to Berra as "my assistant manager," and Yogi had managed the Yankees to a pennant in 1964, so we naturally figured he would be the guy to take over for Stengel. But Casey picked Westrum.
>
> Westrum was supposed to be only an interim manager until Stengel returned, but the next year Casey said, "How will it look if I have to go to the mound with a cane to take out a pitcher?" and he retired. The Mets made Westrum the manager.

Westrum, according to Lang, "wasn't a bad manager. He just had bad players. He was a good guy for the writers, a regular guy who loved to drink his beer and just seemed to fade into the background. One night, I was sitting in a bar with Yogi and Westrum and some fan came over and asked Yogi for his autograph. Berra signed and the guy turned to me, pointed to Westrum and asked, 'Is he anybody?' It seemed to be Westrum's fate to go unnoticed. As a player, he was overshadowed in New York by Yogi with the Yankees and Roy Campanella with the Dodgers."

As a manager, Westrum was placed in the difficult position of succeeding the legendary Stengel. He could never measure up to Casey's unparalleled success with the Yankees, or to Casey's ability to generate publicity and attention, although he did come close to approaching Stengel as a purveyor of unusual dialogue.

"One time in spring training," Lang remembered, "the Mets lost one of those free-for-all games in which the lead changed hands several times. After the game, Westrum's comment was, 'That was a real cliff-dweller.' The Mets were a terrible team under Westrum. They'd find a lot of different ways to lose games and, many times, the writers would go into Westrum's office after another tough loss and the first words out of Wes's mouth were, 'My God, wasn't that awful?'"

Once, when the Mets were in another of their frequent stretches of bad baseball and chronic defeats, Westrum held a clubhouse meeting in which he ripped into his players, blasting them for their indifference and their sloppy play.

"There's too much dissension on this club," he charged, leaving his players, and the writers, to wonder just how much dissension is enough.

Don't be misled by **Wes Westrum**'s career batting average of .217 for 11 major league seasons, all with the Giants. Wes had some pop in his bat. Don't throw him a curveball because he could hit it out of the park, especially in the Polo Grounds with its short left-field porch. He hit 23 homers in 1950 and 20 in 1951.

But Westrum's forte was as an exceptional defensive catcher and an excellent handler of pitchers. He could throw runners out at second and he became very adept at handling Hoyt Wilhelm's knuckleball. In 1950, he set a National League record with a .999 fielding percentage and led NL catchers in assists and double plays.

Westrum was a "Who me?" guy. By that I mean he'd pull some prank and when you looked at him, he'd give you that innocent "Who me?" look. But he was a good guy, and as a catcher he could keep runners off second base. He handled Hoyt Wilhelm's knuckleball as well as anybody, and that was before they started using the oversized mitt.

After his playing career was over, Wes became a coach for the Giants and then was involved in the only trade for coaches in baseball history. Cookie Lavagetto was coaching for the Mets, and Westrum was coaching for the Giants. Cookie was from northern California and he wanted to get back home, so the Mets and Giants agreed to trade coaches. Lavagetto went to the Giants and Westrum went to the Mets, which turned out to be a break for him.

When Casey Stengel broke his hip during the 1965 season, the Mets made Westrum their manager. He held that job through 1967. Unfortunately, the

Wes Westrum is the batter in this photo, stepping aside from the action as teammate
Willie Mays steals home plate during a game against the Cubs in 1951.

Mets were a bad team in those days. In three years under Westrum, they never finished higher than ninth place.

When the Mets let him go, Wes returned to the Giants and wound up being named their manager for the second half of 1974 and 1975. In San Francisco, he did a little better than he had done with the Mets, finishing in third place in 1975. But I guess it wasn't good enough, because in 1976 Westrum was replaced by another of my old New York teammates, Bill Rigney.

Statistical Summaries

All statistics are for player's Giants career only.

HITTING

G = Games

H = Hits

HR = Home runs

RBI = Runs batted in

SB = Stolen bases

BA = Batting average

Catcher	Years	G	H	HR	RBI	SB	BA
Roger Bresnahan *As a pitcher, tossed a shutout in his first major league start for Washington on August 27, 1897*	1902–08	751	731	15	291	118	.293
Walker Cooper *Eight-time All-Star between 1942 and 1950*	1946–49	360	340	63	243	3	.276
Shanty Hogan *Led NL catchers with .966 fielding percentage in 1931*	1928–32	618	627	48	333	4	.311

continued	Years	G	H	HR	RBI	SB	BA
Ernie Lombardi *Hit four home runs as a pinch-hitter in 1947*	1943–47	472	398	55	239	1	.288
Wes Westrum *Drew 104 walks in 1951*	1947–57	919	503	96	315	10	.217

FIELDING

PO = Putouts

A = Assists

E = Errors

DP = Double plays

TC/G = Total chances divided by games played

FA = Fielding average

Catcher	PO	A	E	DP	TC/G	FA
Roger Bresnahan	2,170	506	63	43	6.4	.977
Walker Cooper	1,293	128	32	16	4.5	.978
Shanty Hogan	2,052	275	37	42	4.2	.984
Ernie Lombardi	1,429	179	40	36	6.2	.976
Wes Westrum	3,639	415	62	82	4.6	.985

TWO

First Baseman

Some baseball players have highways named after them, or streets, or schools, or Little League fields, or even bridges. **Willie McCovey** is the only baseball player I know who has a body of water named after him.

"McCovey Cove" lies beyond the right-field fence at SBC Park, a portion of San Francisco Bay that used to be known as China Basin. McCovey Cove is the landing spot for many of Barry Bonds's home runs and, if he were still playing today, would be for McCovey, probably the most feared power hitter of his time. Pitchers like Tom Seaver and first basemen like Keith Hernandez actually have said that when McCovey was at bat, they felt physical fear; that's how hard Willie hit the ball.

When the Giants moved to San Francisco in 1958, they brought with

1. WILLIE McCOVEY

2. BILL TERRY

3. ORLANDO CEPEDA

4. JOHNNY MIZE

5. WHITEY LOCKMAN

them most of the players who had been their core in New York, Whitey Lockman, Danny O'Connell, Daryl Spencer, Hank Sauer, Johnny Antonelli, Stu Miller, Ruben Gomez, and, of course, the great Willie Mays.

Although he was still a great player, still in the prime of his career, Mays was not an immediate fan favorite in San Francisco, probably because the fans

17

in the Bay Area associated him with New York and they wanted their own hero. When McCovey joined the Giants on July 30, 1959, he became an immediate favorite, helped, no doubt, by the fact that in his first game he had four hits, including two triples, against the Phillies' great Hall of Fame pitcher Robin Roberts.

McCovey batted .354 that season, hit 13 home runs, and drove in 38 and even though he played in only 52 games, he was voted National League

Willie McCovey, shown here in 1979, made a splash in his Giants debut 20 years earlier, going 4-for-4 against future Hall of Famer Robin Roberts.

Rookie of the Year and a Hall of Fame career was launched. In the years that followed, "Stretch" became a greater San Francisco idol than Mays. He stayed with the Giants for the next 14 seasons, leading the league in home runs three times and in RBIs twice. In 1969 he became the fifth player in major league history to lead his league in home runs and RBIs in back-to-back seasons.

In 1962 against the Yankees, McCovey was involved in one of the most memorable moments in World Series history. It was the ninth inning of the seventh game with the Yankees leading, 1–0, when McCovey came to bat against Ralph Terry with two runners on base. Big Mac launched a tremendous drive over the right-field fence that would have landed in McCovey Cove had the game been played in SBC Park. When it left the bat, it looked like a game-ending, Series-winning, three-run homer, but the ball hooked foul by inches at the last moment.

McCovey then hit a blistering line drive that also looked like a game-winning hit when it left the bat. But this time it was grabbed by second baseman Bobby Richardson, playing in short right field, and the Series was over.

Big Mac was traded to the San Diego Padres in 1974 and after three seasons with the Padres and Oakland Athletics, he returned to San Francisco in 1977 and finished out his career with four seasons as a Giant.

When he retired, McCovey had played more years at first base (22) than any player in history, had hit the most home runs ever at Candlestick Park (236, with 231 of them as a Giant), was second to Lou Gehrig in grand slams with 18, and had hit 521 home runs, more than any left-handed hitter in National League history until Barry Bonds passed him in 2001.

Despite his size, 6'4", 200 pounds, and his intimidating presence at the plate, McCovey is one of the gentlest people you could meet, soft-spoken and humble, and arguably the most beloved San Francisco Giant of them all.

Although I never saw **Bill Terry** play, I did get to know him slightly when I joined the Giants in 1946. At the time, Terry had the title of general manager and was in charge of the farm system.

I didn't get to know Terry well. I didn't spend a lot of time with him. Bill was kind of aloof and standoffish, which is how players, writers, and fans perceived him in his days on the field.

Despite his reputation, Terry was a towering figure in the history of Giants baseball, both as a player and a manager.

Bill Terry was the best defensive first baseman of his era and drove in 100 or more runs in six straight seasons (1927–1932).

The story goes that a friend had told John McGraw about a young man with exceptional talent as a hitter and a pitcher playing for Memphis. In the spring of 1923, after the Giants broke training camp and headed home, they stopped in Memphis during an exhibition tour on their way north. McGraw took advantage of the opportunity to meet with a brash, young Terry.

"They tell me you're quite a ballplayer," McGraw said.

"That's what they tell me, too," Terry replied.

"How would you like to come to New York with me and play for the Giants?"

"For how much?" Terry asked.

McGraw was taken aback by Terry's reaction.

"If that's the way you feel about it," he said, "take your time and think it over."

In spite of himself, something about young Terry's attitude, and his indifference, appealed to McGraw, especially since Terry had come so highly recommended. Two weeks later, McGraw sent Terry a telegram with a generous offer. Terry accepted and headed to New York, where McGraw worked him out as a pitcher and first baseman.

McGraw found Terry lacking the stuff to make it in the major leagues as a pitcher, but he was impressed with Terry's hitting ability and sent the youngster to Toledo to play first base. Terry returned in 1924, played in 77 games and batted .239, but in the World Series against Washington, he hit a robust .429. The following season, McGraw shifted Long George Kelly to second base and handed the first baseman's job to Terry, where he remained for 12 great seasons.

Although he was big enough, 6'1", 200 pounds, and strong enough to easily reach the short right-field seats in the Polo Grounds, only 257 feet away down the line, Terry's style was to hit the ball where it was pitched and find the alleys. In his career, he hit almost as many triples (112) as home runs (154). He hit double figures in home runs only six times, more than 20 only three times. But he was an outstanding, slashing hitter, a big run producer who drove in more than 100 runs for six consecutive seasons from 1927 to 1932, and the finest defensive first baseman of his time, with exceptional range. He led National League first basemen in fielding percentage twice, double plays three times, putouts and assists five times, and total chances per game nine times.

He batted over .300 in each of his last 10 years, hit over .340 six times, and finished with a career batting average of .341. His 1930 season was one of the best in baseball history, with 39 doubles, 15 triples, 23 home runs, 129 RBIs, 254 hits, and a batting average of .401.

Critics point out that 1930 was "the year of the hitter," with the entire National League batting .303. What those critics fail to mention is that there were 30 other future Hall of Famers playing in the major leagues in 1930, such as all-time greats Al Simmons, Lou Gehrig, Babe Ruth, Mickey Cochrane, George Sisler, Kiki Cuyler, Charlie Gehringer, and Jimmie Foxx, and Terry was the only one to bat over .401. Almost 80 years have passed and Terry and Ted Williams (.406 in 1941) are the only hitters to have reached the .400 mark.

Terry continued to be a productive hitter even after he succeeded McGraw as manager during the 1932 season and became a player/manager. In his final season, reduced to a part-time player and full-time manager, he batted .310 and brought the Giants their first of two consecutive pennants.

I'll talk about Bill Terry's "second career" with the Giants in the chapter on managers.

Imagine the dilemma facing the Giants in 1960. They had two young, power-hitting first basemen, both of whom had been voted National League Rookie of the Year, **Orlando Cepeda** in 1958 and Willie McCovey in 1959, and both of whom would eventually be elected to the Hall of Fame. It was an embarrassment of riches.

Cepeda arrived in San Francisco as a 20-year-old and became an instant hit in his first major league game when he beat the hated Dodgers with a home run off Don Drysdale. Cepeda's father had been a huge star in Puerto Rico known as "the Bull," so Orlando became "the Baby Bull" in San Francisco. Bill Rigney called him "the best young right-handed power hitter I've ever seen."

When McCovey arrived in 1959, the Giants were faced with a problem, which they attempted to resolve by trying both players in the outfield. In 1959, Cepeda played 44 games in the outfield. In 1960, he was in the outfield for 91 games, in 1961 for 80 games. In 1962, McCovey played 57 games in the outfield, in 1963 he played 135 games in the outfield, and in 1964 he was an outfielder for 83 games.

Eventually, the Giants realized one of the two had to go, so on May 8, 1966, Cepeda was traded to the Cardinals for left-hander Ray Sadecki.

When he left, "Cha Cha" had hit 226 home runs, driven in 767 runs, and batted over .300 six times in seven full seasons with the Giants. He had driven

Orlando Cepeda slides safely into third base against the Dodgers during a game in 1963. He was eventually dealt to St. Louis in 1966 but remains one of the greatest Giants of all time.

in more than 100 runs three times, hit more than 30 homers four times, and in 1961 led the National League in home runs with 46 and in RBIs with 142.

In St. Louis, Cepeda picked up where he had left off in San Francisco, being named Most Valuable Player in 1967, when he batted .325, hit 25 homers, and led the league with 111 RBIs.

Later Cepeda moved on to the Braves and Red Sox and continued to be a productive hitter until he retired after the 1974 season with 379 homers, 1,365 RBIs, and a .297 batting average, good enough to be elected to the Hall of Fame in 1999, only the second native Puerto Rican so honored (Roberto Clemente was the first).

Eventually, Cepeda returned to San Francisco, where he makes his home and is currently employed by the Giants as "community representative," known and admired as an ambassador for baseball and for his humanitarian efforts.

Those who remember **Johnny Mize** as the big, lumbering, power-hitting first baseman for the Giants, and later as the pinch-hitter deluxe for the Yankees, may be surprised to learn that in his early days with the Cardinals, he was one of the best average hitters in the National League, and that he led the league with 16 triples in 1938 and with 39 doubles in 1941.

In his first four seasons, Mize batted .329, .364, .337, and a league-leading .349, drove in more than 100 runs three times, and had fewer than 50 strikeouts three times. He had the rare combination of a high batting average and power. He led the league in homers in 1939 and 1940.

After one year with the Giants—he came in 1942, in a trade for three players plus $50,000—he became a different kind of hitter. He spent three years in the navy during World War II, and when he returned in 1946, he was 33 years old and he had slowed considerably. He couldn't run very well, but once he got going, I was amazed that he could roll around those bases pretty good for a big guy. Like a barrel. And he still could hit, not for as high an average as in his Cardinals days, but for power.

I guess he realized he had slowed down and he took one look at that cozy right-field fence in the Polo Grounds, just 257 feet down the line, and decided he would go for the long ball. He didn't need the Polo Grounds to hit the ball out of the park—he could hit the ball out of any park—but he used the Polo Grounds to his advantage. He had big arms and could get on top of the ball with that big lumber and hook the outside pitch into the seats down the line.

24

Not many, when they talk about the greatest hitters of all time, will bring up the name Johnny Mize. The "Big Cat" is best remembered as a pinch-hitter deluxe for the five-time world champion Yankees of 1949–53, or as one of the two premier home-run hitters in the National League with the New York Giants in 1947–48.

But there was another Johnny Mize, a keen-eyed, sweet-swinging, high-average Johnny Mize, who never batted lower than .314 in his first six major league seasons with the St. Louis Cardinals, who led the National League in batting in 1939 with a .349 average, who led the league in doubles with 39 in 1941 and in triples with 16 in 1938.

It's to that Johnny Mize that no less an authority than Ted Williams, "the greatest hitter that ever lived" according to many, paid homage at his "Ted Williams Hitters Museum" in Hernando, Florida.

In conjunction with the museum, Williams, in 1995, produced a video and a companion book in which he selects baseball's 20 greatest hitters of all time, humbly recusing himself from such scrutiny.

"We researched every hitter that I could think of, every hitter that I had ever heard was a great hitter," Williams said. "And we had a research team that wouldn't quit. We had a formula that was absolutely foolproof. They're using some things now that they never used before. One is percentage of times on base per times at bat.

"A fellow that gets a lot of walks isn't given enough credit. Some guy hits .360. Another guy hits .330, but you put his walks in there and he's a .380 hitter."

On Williams's list of the top 20, Johnny Mize is ranked number 15, just behind Al Simmons and just ahead of Mel Ott.

Williams: "I was impressed immediately that he didn't swing and miss too often (only 524 strikeouts in 6,443 at-bats). I was also impressed that he didn't swing at bad balls (856 walks) and he still hit a ton of home runs (359 in 15 seasons), 51 of them in one year (1947).

"I always thought he was one of the very best hitters I saw and I did see Johnny Mize."

Enos Slaughter (a St. Louis Cardinals teammate of Mize's from 1938 to 1941): "Johnny Mize, with his bat, was a valuable member of the ballclub. He had keen eyes. Very seldom did he swing at a bad ball."

Ralph Kiner (number 20 on Williams's hit list and Mize's chief challenger as National League home-run king in the mid-1940s; they finished tied for the league lead in homers in 1947 and '48): "Mize was a great, great hitter. In my book, you have to put him up there with the great hitters of all-time, not only as a power hitter but as a contact hitter as well. The amazing thing about him is that he was a tough guy to strike out.

"In St. Louis, he was a great average hitter who used the whole field. It wasn't until he was traded to the Giants that Mize changed his style of hitting to take advantage of the dimensions of the Polo Grounds. It had a huge center field, more than 450 feet away, and the power alleys were deep, but it was only 258 feet down the right-field line, so Mize waited on the ball and became a pull hitter and a big home-run threat."

That's another thing that has changed in baseball from when I played. Back then, the big, strong power hitters used heavy bats. Today, all the home-run hitters use light bats that they can whip and generate bat speed.

I remember playing in an old-timers game at Shea Stadium. It was my turn at bat and somebody said, "Hey, Thomson, get a bat." So I grabbed an extra heavy bat and I walked up to the plate.

Yogi Berra was catching and they brought in Whitey Ford, so I said to Yogi, "Why do they have to bring him in to pitch to me?"

I got up there just trying to survive. I'm thinking, "Just don't strike out, hit the ball." Whitey threw me a pitch and I made contact and the ball sailed out of the park, a home run. I think it was more the bat than me. The ball just bounced off the bat.

After the game, we were in the locker room and Whitey came up to me and said, "You SOB," and he reached up to choke me. Just then, somebody walked by and said, "Hey, Whitey, when did Ralph Branca teach you how to pitch to Thomson?"

Back to Mize. In 1947, the year the Giants set the National League record with 221 homers, he tied Ralph Kiner for the league lead in home runs with 51 and led the league in RBIs with 138. In 1948, Mize again tied Kiner for the league lead in homers with 40 and drove in 125 runs.

Mize is one of only two players to hit three home runs in a game six times (Sammy Sosa is the other), and he also had 24 games of two home runs.

The 1949 season would be Mize's last as a full-time player. When Leo Durocher took over as manager of the Giants, he wanted to stress youth, speed, and defense, so he started unloading the older, slower players like

Johnny Mize (far right; that's me on the left and Willard Marshall in the middle, by the way) epitomized that rare combination of a power hitter who could also bat .320 or better.

Walker Cooper, Willard Marshall, Sid Gordon, and Mize, who was sold to the Yankees in August. With the Yankees, Mize was a part-time first baseman and a dangerous and effective pinch-hitter in each of their five straight World Series championships from 1949 to 1953. For three straight years, from 1951 to 1953, he led the American League in pinch-hits.

He may have been a good first baseman in his early days, but when I played with him, he wasn't very mobile. I remember one game in 1947, I was playing second base and I had a pretty good arm. I fielded a ground ball and threw it to first base, about four feet off the ground. Mize reached out and the ball went right past his glove. He never touched it, and they gave me an error. He was not a great first baseman when I saw him, but he could hit.

Mize was a student of hitting. He had excellent plate discipline, a keen eye and a great idea of the strike zone. He struck out only 524 times in 15 seasons. Like Ted Williams, he wouldn't swing at a pitch out of the strike zone. He'd rather take ball four than swing at a pitch that wasn't a strike. Because of his reputation as a hitter and a guy who wouldn't swing at pitches out of the strike zone, Mize usually got the benefit of the doubt from umpires. A pitch that was a half-inch outside, umpires would call a strike on me, but a ball on Mize. That burned me up.

When Mize was inducted into the Hall of Fame in 1981, Stan Musial said of him, "Did you ever see a pitcher knock him down at the plate? Remember how he reacted when he was brushed back? He'd just lean back on his left foot, bend his body back, and let the pitch go by. Then he'd lean back into the batter's box and resume his stance, as graceful as a big cat."

And that was John's nickname, "the Big Cat."

It seems that for a good part of my career I found myself following **Whitey Lockman.** In 1949, when Leo Durocher moved me from left field, I replaced Whitey in center field. In that 1951 playoff game against the Dodgers, I batted sixth, behind Whitey, who batted fifth.

The Giants have had five first basemen who made the Hall of Fame, and four of them are the top four in my list of the best Giants first basemen. The fifth Hall of Famer is "Long" George Kelly.

I suppose baseball historians and anybody who saw Kelly play probably would say that "Long" George deserves a place on my team for his .297 lifetime batting average, four seasons knocking in more than 100 runs, and three seasons hitting more than 20 homers in the so-called dead-ball era.

Whitey Lockman (right), shown here teasing Willie Mays with the help of Leo Durocher (left), didn't have flashy numbers, but if you saw him play every day you appreciated how good he was. *Photo courtesy of Time Life Pictures/Getty Images.*

Others might argue the fifth spot should go to Will Clark, who batted over .300 four times, hit more than 20 home runs four times, and drove in more than 100 runs three times in his eight seasons as a Giant.

But I'm invoking my editorial privilege by picking Whitey Lockman as the Giants' number five first baseman despite his career batting average of .279, 114 home runs, and 563 runs batted in. Lockman was, after all, my teammate, my longtime roommate with the Giants, and, to this day, one of my closest friends.

However, it's not only out of friendship that I have chosen Lockman. He didn't dazzle you with numbers, but he was steady. You had to see him play on a daily basis to appreciate Whitey as a ballplayer, and I saw him every day for six years. He was a clutch and consistent hitter, an outstanding fielder, and, most important, a winner.

You need only to know that it was Lockman's double in the ninth inning of that 1951 playoff game that knocked Don Newcombe out of the game and put the tying runs on base and gave me my chance to hit. I shudder to think of what might have happened if Whitey didn't get the double and I went up there with two out.

Lockman's real name was Carroll Walter, a good ol' boy from North Carolina, but only on occasion did anyone call him Carroll. He was Whitey to us. He came up to the Giants as an outfielder and it was in the outfield that he played in the first four years of his major league career. Then in May 1951, Leo Durocher moved him to first base. It was a chain reaction of moves by Leo, primarily to accommodate Willie Mays, and it strengthened our team in several positions and helped us come from 13½ games behind to win the pennant that year.

Durocher wanted Mays to be his center fielder, which history has proved was the right move. To do that, he moved me from center field to third base and he switched Monte Irvin from first base to left field and he moved Lockman from left field to first base, a position Whitey had never played. It's not easy to switch positions that late in your career, especially going from the outfield to first base, where you're involved in almost every play and there's so much more to do.

Lockman had been an exceptional outfielder. He had speed, but he didn't have a big arm, so that may be why Leo felt he was better suited to first base. And he took to the position like Mark Spitz took to water. He became one of the best fielding first basemen in the league.

Gil Hodges was considered the best defensive first baseman in the league at that time, but for me, there wasn't anything Gil did that Whitey couldn't do. The one thing Hodges had over Lockman was size. Hodges was 6'2", 200 pounds, and he had these huge hands, so big they used to kid him that he didn't even need a glove. Lockman was 6'1", 175 pounds.

I'm taking nothing away from Hodges. He was awfully good, especially on bunts. It was hard to bunt a runner over with Hodges charging. But over the years that I was playing, Whitey handled the glove at first base as well as anybody.

In addition to his clutch hitting and his defense, Lockman was a very heady player, a student of the game and a guy who liked to talk baseball, which we did quite a lot, especially before air travel became the thing and we were taking trains on road trips. We'd sit around and pass the time on those train rides by talking fundamentals. Alvin Dark, Eddie Stanky, Larry Jansen, and Lockman were usually in the middle of those sessions.

Whitey was a baseball guy through and through. When his playing career was over, he went into coaching and got a shot at managing, three years with the Cubs. Later, he scouted for many years for the Cubs.

31

The Giants had quite a few outstanding first basemen over the years. In fact, it might have been their most bountiful position. Consequently, because I'm limited to picking five, I have had to leave off some very deserving players.

To give them their due, I'll mention them here. I've mentioned "Long" George Kelly, one of the big stars in the early days, long before my time, a guy who hit 148 home runs in the days when players were not hitting a lot of home runs, and Will Clark, a lifetime .303 hitter who came after my time. I did get to see him play, mostly on television, and I admired him a great deal. He was a good hitter and an excellent fielder.

There also was Fred Merkle, Babe Young, Phil Weintraub, Bill White, and J.T. Snow, but I'll still stick with my top five choices.

Statistical Summaries

All statistics are for player's Giants career only.

HITTING

G = Games

H = Hits

HR = Home runs

RBI = Runs batted in

SB = Stolen bases

BA = Batting average

First Baseman	Years	G	H	HR	RBI	SB	BA
Willie McCovey *MVP of both the All-Star Game and National League in 1969*	1959–73, 1977–80	2,256	1,974	469	1,388	24	.274
Bill Terry *Hit for the cycle on May 29, 1928*	1923–36	1,721	2,193	154	1,078	56	.341
Orlando Cepeda *Drove in eight runs in 19–3 victory at Chicago on July 4, 1961*	1958–66	1,114	1,286	226	767	92	.308

continued	Years	G	H	HR	RBI	SB	BA
Johnny Mize *Had 30 multiple-home-run games during his career*	1942, 1946–49	655	733	157	505	13	.299
Whitey Lockman *Led off two consecutive games with home runs, July 18 and 19, 1953*	1945, 1947–56	1,485	1,571	113	543	41	.281

FIELDING

PO = Putouts

A = Assists

E = Errors

DP = Double plays

TC/G = Total chances divided by games played

FA = Fielding average

First Baseman	PO	A	E	DP	TC/G	FA
Willie McCovey	14,956	1,058	203	1,213	9.1	.987
Bill Terry	15,972	1,108	138	1,334	11.3	.992
Orlando Cepeda	7,273	494	96	699	9.2	.988
Johnny Mize	5,967	451	44	489	10.0	.993
Whitey Lockman	6,484	497	74	647	9.8	.990

THREE

Second Baseman

Frankie Frisch, "the Fordham Flash." It's one of the great names in New York baseball, just as Frisch is one of the great players in baseball history.

Frisch had a Hall of Fame playing career, 2,880 hits and a lifetime batting average of .316 for 19 major league seasons. A switch-hitter with blinding speed, he hit over .300 13 times, led the league in hits once, and led the league in stolen bases three times, all before my time.

He managed the Cardinals for five and a half seasons and won a pennant and World Series in 1934. Later, he managed the Pirates for seven seasons and the Cubs for two and a half seasons.

The Frankie Frisch I knew was a broadcaster for the Giants, one of the first former players to become a baseball announcer. It was 1947 and Frank had just been fired as manager of the Pirates when Giants owner Horace Stoneham hired him as a broadcaster.

1. FRANKIE FRISCH

2. JEFF KENT

3. LARRY DOYLE

4. BURGESS WHITEHEAD

5. EDDIE STANKY

What a character he was. If a Giants pitcher walked a batter, Frisch would complain on the air, "Oh, those bases on balls!" He was hot stuff. He'd come into the clubhouse after a game and, in that gravelly voice of his, he'd tell us what happened in the game we had just played, as if we didn't know.

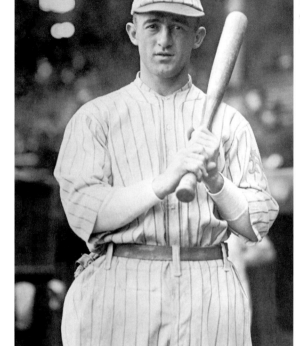

The great Frankie Frisch batted over .300 13 times in his 19-year Hall of Fame career. *Photo courtesy of MLB Photos via Getty Images.*

36

The Giants had a player named Jack Lohrke playing third base that year. His nickname was "Lucky Jack," because when he was with Spokane in the Western International League, Jack was on board the team bus getting ready for a trip when he was called off the bus and informed he had been promoted to Triple A. The bus left 15 minutes later and crashed into a ravine, killing eight players on board.

So "Lucky Jack" was our third baseman and Chesterfield cigarettes was the sponsor of Giants games on radio and television. And, of course, Chesterfield's main competitor was Lucky Strike cigarettes. Now Frisch was broadcasting the games and if Lohrke did something, made a great play or got a big hit, Frisch would say, "There's Lucky Jack." All Frisch had to do was mention Lucky Jack and the phone would ring and the voice on the other end would say, "Hey, Frank...Chesterfield!"

One time we were playing the Cincinnati Reds and I went out for batting practice and there's Frisch sitting on the end of the bench, talking to himself. I said to him, "Hey, Frank, you're talking to yourself."

He looked up and said, "Shut up, I'm practicing pronouncing Kluszewski. Kluszewski…Kluszewski…Kluszewski."

As a player, Frisch was a club owner's dream, a local boy from the Bronx who had been a big star at Fordham University in baseball, football, basketball, and track. The Giants signed him right out of Fordham and he joined the big club in 1919 without ever playing a game in the minor leagues. He struggled that first year, batting only .226 in 54 games, but the next year he hit .280 and then batted over .300 for the next six seasons with the Giants, including .348 in 1923.

John McGraw, who had the reputation of being an excellent judge of young talent, took an immediate liking to Frisch. He liked his speed, his desire, and his athletic ability. McGraw personally took Frisch under his wing, working on Frank's hitting and sliding technique and perfecting his base-stealing ability, helping him become a daring and accomplished base stealer. McGraw even made Frisch team captain.

Frisch played all three infield positions, second, short, and third, wherever McGraw needed him, and was a mainstay on the Giants' four straight National League pennant champions, from 1921 to 1924. In the World Series in those four years, he batted .300, .471, .400, and .333.

Probably Frisch's best attribute as a hitter was his ability to make contact. In 9,112 at-bats, he struck out only 272 times, and only twice in 19 seasons did he strike out more than 18 times. In 1927, for example, he had 208 hits, batted .337, and in 617 at-bats had the same number of strikeouts as home runs, 10.

When the Giants failed to win a fifth straight pennant in 1925 and finished fifth in 1926, McGraw seemed to lay the blame on Frisch, trading him to St. Louis for Rogers Hornsby, the premier hitter in the National League who had had a falling out of his own with Cardinals owner Sam Breadon.

It couldn't have been easy for Frisch replacing a player who had won six consecutive batting titles in St. Louis, hitting a cumulative .397 in that span, but Frank's daring base running, exceptional fielding, and excellent hitting soon helped him win over the fans of St. Louis. In his first season with the Cardinals, he batted .337 and led the league's second basemen in fielding percentage, assists with 641, and total chances with 1,059, both records. It didn't hurt, either, that the Cardinals finished in second place, a half game ahead of the Giants.

With the Cardinals, Frisch would play in four more World Series and, in 1933, he became their player/manager, reaping the benefits of Branch Rickey's lush farm system with players like Dizzy and Paul Dean, Pepper Martin, Leo Durocher, Joe Medwick, and Ripper Collins.

Frisch's own fiery temperament on the ball field made him the perfect leader of that band of raucous, swashbuckling, hard-driving, hell-for-leather battlers known as the Gashouse Gang.

An egotistical jerk. Aloof. Self-centered. A "me first" guy. Unapproachable. A loner. Quick-tempered. Unfriendly. Irascible.

I've heard all those words used to describe **Jeff Kent,** but I don't know about any of that. I don't know the man. What I do know from observing him is that Kent probably will end up being the best run-producing second baseman in baseball history, and that's saying something when you look at the list of second basemen in the Hall of Fame: Rogers Hornsby, Frankie Frisch, Charlie Gehringer, Eddie Collins, Jackie Robinson, Bobby Doerr, Tony Lazzeri, Joe Morgan, and Ryne Sandberg.

Kent already has hit more home runs than any other second baseman in history (he passed Sandberg in 2004 when he hit his 278th) and he's closing in on Hornsby's record for most RBIs as a second baseman.

Another thing I learned about Kent is that he is the son of a California motorcycle cop who rose through the ranks to become a lieutenant and was a demanding parent. From his dad, Jeff learned discipline, competitiveness, a strong work ethic, a desire to be the best at what he does, and a drive to win.

Early in his career, Kent moved around a lot and found only moderate success. He was drafted by the Toronto Blue Jays and soon after reaching the major leagues was traded to the Mets, who couldn't make up their mind where to play him. Second base was his natural position, but the Mets saw his power potential and thought of him as a third baseman. After five mediocre and turbulent seasons in New York, where he was depicted as being anti-social, he was traded to Cleveland, where he spent one season before going to the Giants in a controversial trade.

*I*t takes a manager of a team that has dominated the National League for most of the past two decades to appreciate an opponent.

For all of those years Bobby Cox, manager of the Atlanta Braves who has won more than 2,000 games and is pushing Tony La Russa for third place on the all-time list, behind the legendary Connie Mack and John McGraw, has viewed Jeff Kent up close and personal. And his view from the Braves bench is one of respect, admiration, and fear.

Said Cox:

> *Jeff is getting up in years, but he's a better player now than he was in Toronto or in his first two years with the Mets. He became a great hitter, for me, sort of out of nowhere. He was always a decent hitter, but somehow or another, he became a great hitter. He's a great hitter right now.*
>
> *He started with the Blue Jays a few years after I left there, so I never had him as a manager. But I've seen him do some damage against me as an opponent. He went from Toronto to the Mets and was okay, nothing great. He got the most out of his skills as an infielder, and now he's one of the feared hitters that you face.*

There is little question that Kent rates among the best offensive second basemen the game has known, deserving to be compared with the likes of Charlie Gehringer, Frankie Frisch, Eddie Collins, Tony Lazzeri, Ryne Sandberg, Bobby Doerr, Billy Herman, and even the incomparable Rogers Hornsby. It's been Kent's defense that has been suspect, but Cox doesn't quite see it that way.

In Cox's view, Kent's range is "just average, at best. But he can make the double play. He can turn it and he doesn't shy off, and he's tough. One of the reasons he's still playing second base is his bat. To get the kind of production he gives a team at what is primarily a defensive position is a bonus. I don't think voters look too closely at defense when it comes to being elected to the Hall of Fame or being selected Most Valuable Player."

Does Cox think Kent is a Hall of Famer?

40

Jeff Kent isn't the surest-handed second baseman ever to play the position, but he may go down as the most productive offensively.

"Good question," he replied. "Is Mike Piazza a Hall of Famer? If you say yes, and I think he is, then you have to say yes to Kent for the same reason. He's one of the best offensive players ever at his position.

"Put his offensive numbers alongside people like Joe Morgan, who's in the Hall of Fame, or Roberto Alomar, who I think should be in the Hall of Fame, and you'd have to say that Kent belongs. So I'd have to say yes, Jeff Kent is a Hall of Famer."

In order to get Kent, the Giants gave up Matt Williams, a perennial All-Star, a big run-producer, and one of the most popular players in the Bay Area. The deal was roundly criticized and Giants general manager Brian Sabean took a lot of heat over the trade. He defended himself by stating, "I am not an idiot."

It turned out to be one of the best trades Sabean ever made.

In San Francisco, Kent found a comfort level under manager Dusty Baker, who put Jeff at second base and left him there. Kent responded by finally reaching his potential as a hitter in 1997, his first season as a Giant. Although he batted only .250, he drove in 121 runs and belted 29 homers, three more than Hornsby's previous record for a Giants second baseman. He would spend five more seasons with the Giants and never hit below .290.

His critics are quick to point out that Kent is barely adequate defensively. He doesn't have great range, or the surest hands, but nobody questions his desire or his bat.

Former Giant Kevin Mitchell called him "the best offensive second baseman I've ever seen," and teammate J.T. Snow said, "There's nobody better at hanging in on the double play."

Another former teammate, Rich Aurilia, said, "His emphasis is hustling and playing hard. He might make errors because he goes all out on every play. I don't know anyone who stays in there longer on double plays."

In 1999, Kent became the first Giant in eight years to hit for the cycle. In 2000, he had his career year, a .334 batting average, 33 homers, and 125 RBIs, for which he was voted the National League's Most Valuable Player. He also joined George "Highpockets" Kelly, Irish Meusel, Bill Terry, Mel Ott, Willie Mays, and Barry Bonds as the only Giants to drive in 100 runs for four straight seasons.

When Baker left the Giants to take over as manager of the Cubs in 2002, Kent also walked, signing a free-agent contract with the Houston Astros. But he left his mark in San Francisco. In his six seasons as a Giant, Kent drove in more than 100 runs every year, and averaged 115 RBIs and 29 home runs per season.

Imagine the fear in the heart of 20-year-old **Larry Doyle** on July 22, 1907, his first day in the major leagues, when he took the wrong ferry across the Hudson River and arrived at the Polo Grounds just as the game was about to start. Giants manager John McGraw put Doyle in the starting lineup anyway, but at second base, a position unfamiliar to the youngster.

To add to his eventful day, Doyle booted a crucial ground ball in the ninth inning of a game the Giants lost.

After the game, a sheepish Doyle confronted McGraw, whose reputation as a merciless tyrant preceded him and no doubt reached Doyle. Expecting to be immediately sent back to the minor leagues, Doyle was surprised to hear words of encouragement from McGraw, who saw in the youngster a player of great potential.

Doyle rewarded McGraw's faith by playing an outstanding second base for the remainder of the season and batting a respectable .260. McGraw was renowned for having a keen eye for talent and he was so enamored of Doyle, he named the youngster team captain the following season in only his second year in the majors. Doyle responded with a .308 batting average, his first of five seasons over .300 in eight full years with the Giants.

Doyle's hitting and solid defense helped the Giants win three straight pennants starting in 1911, when he batted .310, led the National League with 25 triples, and was quoted by Damon Runyon with the famous line, "It's great to be young and a Giant."

That year, Doyle also was involved in one of the most controversial plays in World Series history. It came in Game 5 with the Philadelphia Athletics leading the Giants, three games to one. With the score tied, 3–3, the Giants batted in the bottom of the tenth. Doyle led off with a double against Ed Plank and moved to third on a bunt by Fred Snodgrass.

Fred Merkle followed with a long drive to right field and Doyle tagged up at third and slid across home plate with the winning run. Or did he?

Years later, umpire Bill Klem admitted that Doyle's slide carried him inches away from the plate and had the Athletics applied the tag, Klem would have ruled Doyle out. But no tag was ever made, so Klem was not required to make any call, and the Giants were 4–3 winners.

It was all for naught as the Athletics returned to Philadelphia for Game 6 and bombed the Giants, 13–2, for their second straight world championship.

The following year, Doyle had his highest batting average, .330, fifth best in the National League, and again led the Giants to a pennant. But the Giants were again beaten in the World Series, this time by the Red Sox.

In 1915, his last full season with the Giants, Doyle won the National League batting title with a .320 average, the last Giant to win a batting crown

Larry Doyle's start with the Giants was an inauspicious one, but he settled in quickly and wound up having a brilliant career. *Photo courtesy of Bettmann/CORBIS.*

until Bill Terry hit .401 15 years later. Doyle also led the league in hits with 189 and doubles with 40.

In August of the following year, with the Giants having slipped to fourth place, Doyle was traded to the Cubs, where he stayed through the 1917 season and then returned to the Giants in 1918 to finish out his career. He retired after the 1920 season with a lifetime batting average of .290 and 298 stolen bases, including 17 steals of home.

Doyle died at the age of 87 in 1974 in the upstate New York town of Saranac Lake, the same town where Christy Mathewson died almost a half century earlier.

Burgess Whitehead's career was hampered by poor health and cut short by four years in the navy during World War II. In between, he was a slick-fielding second baseman and a capable hitter.

I got to see Whitehead in his last year in the big leagues, 1946, when he was with the Pirates. He was 36 years old at the time and he wasn't the same player he had been earlier, but even then I saw enough to be impressed. He was a very fancy fielder with great footwork.

Old-timers would talk about Charlie Gehringer, the great Tigers second baseman and Hall of Famer, and how beautiful he was to watch. When I saw Whitehead, it put me in mind of Gehringer because he was that kind of second baseman; beautiful to watch and with fancy footwork.

Frail-looking and sickly, Whitehead had played in only 219 games in three years with the Cardinals when Giants manager Bill Terry gave up two veteran players (pitcher Roy Parmelee, a 14-game winner, and first baseman Phil Weintraub) and cash to get him after the 1935 season.

Terry was roundly criticized for giving up so much for a player who had trouble getting on the field, but Terry had the last laugh when Whitehead did not miss a game in each of the next two seasons and shored up the infield defense for a team that won consecutive pennants. Whitehead led National League second basemen in total chances in 1936 and in putouts, fielding percentage, and double plays in 1937, and he batted .278 and .286, scored 163 runs, and drove in 99 in the two years, to boot.

Illness caused him to miss the entire 1938 season and he never again was able to duplicate his 1936–37 numbers. He wound up playing nine seasons with a career batting average of .266, but his numbers would have been much better if not for poor health and the four years he missed because of military duty.

Burgess Whitehead (fifth from right) looks down in shock at an unconscious Dizzy Dean, whom he'd struck in the head with a line drive on July 14, 1936. Dean recovered fully.

That's Eddie Stanky (far left) running in to congratulate me after the "shot heard 'round the world." He was a Giant for only two years, but he was the "glue of the club," as Durocher called him.

Most baseball fans have seen the film of the home run that beat the Dodgers in the third and final game of the 1951 National League playoff and one thing they surely remember is **Eddie Stanky** running all the way down to the third-base coach's box and wrestling Leo Durocher to the ground in celebration. That little film clip says as much about Stanky as anything; he was a winner, a guy who hated to lose.

A lot of people might not understand the choice of Stanky among the five best Giants second basemen. He was a Giant only two seasons, 1950 and 1951, but in those two years, the Giants won 184 games and a pennant after winning only 73 games the year before he arrived. He had won a pennant with the Dodgers in 1947 and with the Braves in 1948, so he knew about winning.

Durocher called Stanky "the glue of the ballclub." In his two seasons as the Giants' leadoff batter, he had 285 hits, drew 271 walks, and scored 203 runs.

Stanky was "the Brat." If he was your opponent, you hated him; if he was your teammate, you loved him, and I knew him both as an opponent and as a teammate.

When I first came to the Giants in 1946, I was playing second base and Stanky was with the Dodgers. In those days, we used to leave our gloves on the field when we came to bat. When it was time to go on defense, I'd go out to the field and I could never find my glove, and then all of a sudden it would come flying at me from some place. Well, I got sick of that, so after the third out was made, I'd run in real fast to the dugout and turn around and look at the field to see what was happening to my glove. And sure enough, I would see Stanky kicking it into the right-field corner.

That was Eddie Stanky, "the Brat." He'd do anything to win, and I mean anything. He could really get under your skin, really irritate you…unless he was on your side.

I didn't know what to think when we got Stanky and Al Dark from the Braves for four veteran players before the 1950 season. I had had that unpleasant experience with Stanky when he played for the Dodgers, but I soon realized that what Stanky brought with him was a fire and a feistiness, a desire and a will to win, and a lot of baseball knowledge.

Stanky could be snide and he had a way of strutting around with an air of superiority. But he was always trying to fire up guys. In 1951 when we were making our move in August with a 16-game winning streak, before each game Stanky would offer words of encouragement in his own wise guy manner. He'd admonish us, "Hey, you're not playing for your life. Loosen up." And when we had our winning streak stopped, it was Stanky who cost us the game when he booted a ball at second base.

Stanky was like a Durocher clone. They had a history that dated back to their days when they won a pennant with the Dodgers. And after I hit the home run, it was interesting that the first thing Stanky did was head for Durocher in the third-base coach's box.

After the 1951 season, Stanky was traded to the Cardinals, who wanted him to be their manager. Because of the way he played the game, getting by without a great deal of natural ability, everybody assumed he would make an outstanding manager. But he never did live up to people's expectations. He did all right in his first two years with the Cardinals, finishing third both times. But he managed five more years for the Cardinals and the White Sox and never finished higher than fourth.

It's interesting to take note of three Giants second basemen who don't make my list—Rogers Hornsby, Red Schoendienst, and Joe Morgan, all great players, Hall of Famers. But Hornsby played with the Giants only one year and Schoendienst and Morgan only two years, both on the down side of their careers.

Statistical Summaries

All statistics are for player's Giants career only.

HITTING

G = Games

H = Hits

HR = Home runs

RBI = Runs batted in

SB = Stolen bases

BA = Batting average

Second Baseman	Years	G	H	HR	RBI	SB	BA
Frankie Frisch *Had 12 assists in a 10-inning game on August 21, 1923*	1919–26	1,000	1,303	54	524	224	.321
Jeff Kent *Hit three home runs and drove in seven runs in 2002 World Series*	1997–2002	900	1,021	175	689	57	.297
Larry Doyle *Stole four bases on September 18, 1911*	1907–16, 1918–20	1,622	1,751	67	725	291	.292

continued	Years	G	H	HR	RBI	SB	BA
Burgess Whitehead *Had a league leading 141 singles in 1940*	1936–41	650	672	16	182	38	.268
Eddie Stanky *Led all major league players with .460 on-base percentage in 1950*	1950–51	297	285	22	94	17	.274

FIELDING

PO = Putouts

A = Assists

E = Errors

DP = Double plays

TC/G = Total chances divided by games played

FA = Fielding average

Second Baseman	PO	A	E	DP	TC/G	FA
Frankie Frisch	1,469	2,219	110	353	6.1	.971
Jeff Kent	1,745	2,351	81	581	4.9	.981
Larry Doyle	3,316	4,272	409	630	5.0	.949
Burgess Whitehead	1,520	1,871	96	378	6.3	.972
Eddie Stanky	763	830	38	245	5.6	.977

FOUR

Shortstop

Despite winning three consecutive National League pennants from 1921 to 1923, John McGraw knew his Giants were getting old, and so, with his still-keen eye for young talent, he began to retool his team.

Travis Jackson, a 20-year-old Arkansan, was installed as McGraw's short-stop replacing the departed Davey Bancroft. McGraw found more playing time for Bill Terry with an eye toward making him his regular first baseman in place of Long George Kelly, and began the transformation of Freddie Lindstrom from second base with the plan to have him replace Heinie Groh at third base. A slugging right fielder named Mel Ott and pitchers Freddie Fitzsimmons and Carl Hubbell would follow soon after.

1. TRAVIS JACKSON

2. ALVIN DARK

3. DAVE BANCROFT

4. DICK BARTELL

5. BUDDY KERR

Together these youngsters represented McGraw's last hurrah.

Jackson, who had played in 99 games as a utility man in the 1922 and 1923 seasons, was an immediate hit as the Giants' regular shortstop in 1924. He played in 151 games, batted .302, and was a sure-handed fielder with great range and a powerful throwing arm. And he helped the Giants win their fourth straight pennant.

Jackson would hold down the shortstop job for 11 seasons, until 1935, when his range diminished as a result of his age and a knee injury. He was moved to third base, where he played the final two years of his career, and was replaced at shortstop by Dick Bartell.

In 15 seasons, all with the Giants, Jackson batted over .300 six times, with a high of .339 in 1930; hit 135 home runs, with a high of 21 in 1929; drove in 929 runs, with a high of 101 in 1934; and posted a career batting average of .291.

As a shortstop, Jackson led the league twice in fielding average, twice in double plays, and four times in assists.

Travis Jackson was a Hall of Famer who spent his whole career with the Giants, 11 years of it as their everyday shortstop. *Photo courtesy of MLB Photos via Getty Images.*

When his playing days were over, Jackson coached for the Giants and managed in the minor leagues for years. He was elected to the Hall of Fame in 1982 and died five years later, at the age of 83, in the town of his birth, Waldo, Arkansas.

The trade that turned the Giants into champions of the National League in 1951 (of course, that was also the year we had a rookie named Willie Mays) was made after the 1949 season when they sent veterans Willard Marshall, Sid Gordon, Buddy Kerr, and Red Webb to the Boston Braves for their double-play combination of Eddie Stanky and **Alvin Dark.**

Dark had batted .322 and was Rookie of the Year for the Braves in 1948, but in two full seasons he had hit only six home runs in more than 1,000 at-bats. Hitting in the Polo Grounds with its short left-field porch, Dark became a dangerous hitter. In the next five seasons, he belted 87 homers, drove in 70 runs or more three times, batted .300 or higher three times, and helped the Giants win two pennants and one World Series. He also was a reliable and sure-handed fielding shortstop who made all the routine plays, and some spectacular ones, too.

In 1969 fans voted Dark the number one shortstop in Giants history. I have no quarrel with that, but Travis Jackson is in the Hall of Fame and Dark isn't, so I'm making Al number two on my list of all-time Giants shortstops.

Dark was an especially tough hitter in the clutch and you need only look at the ninth inning of the third game of the 1951 playoff against the Dodgers to attest to that. In case you don't remember, I'll remind you that we came to bat in the bottom of the ninth trailing the Dodgers and Don Newcombe, 4–1. Dark led off the inning. Instead of trying to hit the ball out of the park against Newcombe, who was still throwing hard, he slapped the ball the other way and drove a single past a diving Gil Hodges into right field.

Who knows what might have happened if Dark didn't get a rally started with that single? Don Mueller might not have followed with a single past Hodges, who was holding Dark on first, Newcombe might not have left the game, and there might never have been a game-winning, pennant-winning three-run home run by some guy who was born in Glasgow, Scotland.

Dark was as great a competitor as any player I've ever been around, and it showed in that playoff. In the second game when the Dodgers whipped us, 10–0, Dark got into it with Charlie Dressen, the Dodgers manager, who was

53

Alvin Dark, shown here scoring on an inside-the-park home run, played in two World Series with the Giants and later managed them to another.

coaching at third base. Dressen used to like to get on the other team, especially when he was winning, and this day he was chirping pretty good. It got to the point that Dark just couldn't take it any more and he started giving it back to Dressen. I'm standing there at third base listening to them going back and forth, Dark from shortstop to my left, Dressen in the third-base coach's box to my right. It was the only time in all the years I knew him that I ever heard Dark say a swear word.

Dark batted .303 in 1951, drove in 69 runs, hit 14 homers, led the league with 41 doubles, stole 12 bases, and led all National League shortstops in putouts, assists, and double plays. In other words, he was an all-around player.

Dark batted .300 in each of the next two seasons and .293 in 1954, when the Giants won another pennant and swept the Indians in the World Series. In two World Series with the Giants, Alvin was 17-for-41, an average of .415.

One is a black man, born in Alabama and raised in New Jersey. The other is a white man, born in Oklahoma and raised in Louisiana.

In background and culture, they had very little in common. Had their paths crossed at an early age, they would have been polar opposites, drank from different water fountains, used different rest rooms, occupied seats in different sections of the bus, eaten in different restaurants, lived in separate hotels. Had they served together in the military, they would have been segregated, assigned to different units.

The only reason they even met was baseball, which was their common bond. Even that almost never happened.

Monte Irvin had spent 11 years playing in the Negro Leagues, despairing that the opportunity to display his playing talent in front of a wide audience in the major leagues, would never come. But it did come for him, finally, in 1949, at the age of 30, two years after Jackie Robinson had broken the game's color barrier in Brooklyn.

At the time, Alvin Dark, a former star football player at Louisiana State University, was 27 and in his second season with the Boston Braves, a budding star at shortstop.

One year later, Dark was traded by Boston to the New York Giants. He and Irvin became teammates and they would remain so for six seasons.

In 1951, they were vital, integral parts of the greatest comeback in baseball history, helping the Giants come from 13½ games behind the Dodgers in August to force the National League's second playoff. They then helped the Giants beat the Dodgers, two games to one, in the playoff, reaching the World Series against the Yankees. Three years after that, they helped the Giants win the National League pennant by five games over the Dodgers (Dark, a .293 hitter with 20 home runs and 70 RBIs; Irvin—by then 35 years old, nearing the end of the line, slowed by a broken ankle he sustained two years before—batting .262 as a part-time player with 19 homers and 64 RBIs), and win the World Series in a four-game sweep of the Cleveland Indians.

Of Dark, Irvin said:

Alvin was a great player. He was a great captain. And Alvin was a
pretty good hitter, better than he's given credit for. I played with him

for six years and all that stuff that broke when he was managing the Giants, about Alvin being a racist, was never evident when I played with him. We always got along fine. Willie Mays spoke very highly of him and, when the story broke, they asked Jackie Robinson about it and Jackie said the same thing. He had high praise for Alvin.

And Alvin was a great competitor. Remember, he got the hit leading off the bottom of the ninth inning in the third game of the 1951 playoffs against the Dodgers that started our four-run rally. And he got a lot of key hits in the World Series against the Yankees and batted over .400 (.417, 10-for-24, four RBIs), and in the World Series against Cleveland (.412, 7-for-17).

I think he's one of the guys who has been overlooked. I think he belongs in the Hall of Fame. I've always said that. I hope one day he'll make it.

Although he was traded before the Giants left New York and never played for them in San Francisco, he did return to the Giants in California as their manager in 1961, and led them to a pennant in 1962, the Giants' first pennant in eight years. Later, he won a pennant and World Series managing for Charlie Finley in Oakland.

Regrettably, Dark is remembered by many for an unfortunate remark he made when he was managing the Giants. He said something that appeared to question the desire of some black players. It was widely circulated and it branded him as a racist. I believe it was simply a case of Dark expressing some misconceptions that stem from his Louisiana upbringing.

I spent a lot of time around Alvin with the Giants. We had black players on those teams, and never once did I see or hear any indication that Al was a racist.

Dave Bancroft played 16 major league seasons, but only three and a half of them with the Giants. Had he been with them longer, he would rate higher than third on my all-time list of Giants shortstops; he was that good. In his time, most observers rated him a better shortstop than the Braves' Rabbit Maranville, which meant he was the best.

Getting Bancroft was one of John McGraw's best trades. McGraw sent an aging Art Fletcher and a pitcher named Hubbell (not 253-game winner Carl, but 40-game winner Bill, no relation) and cash to the Phillies for Bancroft. At 29, he was in his sixth year as the Phillies' shortstop and in the prime of his career. But the Phillies were in the process of selling off their best players and McGraw jumped right in to land Bancroft.

In his three full seasons with the Giants, Bancroft batted .318, .321, and .304, and played a brilliant short-stop, leading the league in putouts, assists, and double plays in his first two years. He also had six hits in a game in 1920 and hit for the cycle in 1921. The Giants won pennants all three years Bancroft was their shortstop.

In Dave Bancroft's time, most observers rated him a better shortstop than the Braves' Rabbit Maranville, which meant he was the best.

After the '23 season, McGraw traded Bancroft to Boston and floated the story that he was giving up the league's best shortstop as a favor to his old friend, Christy Mathewson, the Braves president, and to

Dave Bancroft (second from left) is shown with his infield mates (from left, Heinie Groh, Frankie Frisch, and "Long" George Kelly) prior to the 1922 season, when they were widely considered the best infield in baseball. *Photo courtesy of Bettmann/CORBIS.*

57

Bancroft, who would become a player/manager for the Braves. The truth was that Bancroft was an aging 32 and McGraw had a 20-year-old replacement named Travis Jackson ready to take over as the Giants' shortstop.

While Bancroft continued to perform at a high level as a player for the Braves, batting over .300 two more times, he was a bust as a manager. In four years, his Braves finished eighth, fifth, seventh, and seventh, and Bancroft was fired. When his playing career was over, Bancroft managed in the minor leagues, but never got a second chance to manage in the majors. He was elected to the Hall of Fame in 1971, the year before he died.

John McGraw would have loved **Dick Bartell,** who was called "Rowdy Dick." He was a throwback, a scrapper, and a battler out of McGraw's "Old Oriole" school, who battled opponents and umpires with his mouth and his fists.

But McGraw was gone when Bartell arrived with the Giants in 1935 after four seasons each with the Pirates and Phillies. He broke in with the Pirates, who kept Bartell instead of a young Joe Cronin, who would wind up in the Hall of Fame.

In New York, Bartell replaced Travis Jackson at shortstop just as Jackson had replaced Dave Bancroft, giving the Giants a streak of 18 consecutive years of outstanding play from three shortstops. It's no coincidence that in those 18 seasons, the Giants won seven pennants.

His aggressiveness that made him such an asset on the playing field also was Bartell's undoing. Wherever he went, he eventually wore out his welcome. He seemed to have a shelf life of four years before teams tired of his volatility. He lasted four years in Pittsburgh, four years in Philadelphia, and four years in New York before moving on to the Cubs for one year and the Tigers for one year.

Dick Bartell was a throwback, a scrapper, and a battler out of McGraw's "Old Oriole" school, who battled opponents and umpires with his mouth and his fists.

In 1941, Bartell returned to the Giants and, with major league rosters depleted by players serving in the military during World War II, managed to eke out four more major league seasons as a utility player.

Later he became a coach with the Giants, and he was there when I had my first workout with the Giants when I was still in high school. I was a shortstop back then, and I remember Rowdy Dick yelling at me, "Hey, okay, shortstop, haul ass," and I guess that told me what kind of player he must have been.

"Rowdy" Dick Bartell (left) poses with the Yankees' Jake Powell before Game 5 of the 1936 World Series. Both players were leading their respective teams in batting average at this time in the Series. *Photo courtesy of Bettmann/CORBIS.*

Buddy Kerr, as slick-fielding a shortstop as there was in his time, fields a pickoff attempt at second base as Jackie Robinson of the Dodgers slides safely back to the base. *Photo courtesy of Bettmann/CORBIS.*

In recent years, when somebody did something to win a World Series or a pennant or a Super Bowl, invariably the first telephone call he would get in the locker room would be from the president of the United States. When I hit the home run against the Dodgers in the third game of the 1951 playoff, the first call I got was from **Buddy Kerr.**

I had just arrived in the locker room and the place was filling up fast with members of the media, employees of the Giants, and various friends and well-wishers. As soon as I got in there, Eddie Logan, our clubhouse man, said, "Bobby, somebody wants you on the telephone." I picked it up and it was Kerr. He was living in the New York area and he had followed the game, either on radio or television, and he called me right away.

Buddy kept laughing, "Hey, hoot mon," he said, and he just kept laughing.

Kerr had been the Giants' shortstop when I first came up in 1946, and I was really impressed with him. I can remember him making one play, going into the hole between short and third, grabbing the ball barehanded, and throwing the runner out at first. I had never seen anybody make that play before, so to me he was a pretty good ballplayer. He wasn't much of a hitter—he had a lifetime average of .249 and the most home runs he ever hit in one season was nine in 1944—but he was as good a defensive shortstop as anybody around in his time.

Buddy was a local boy, from Astoria, Queens, who took over as the Giants' shortstop from another native New Yorker, Billy Jurges, and became one of the slickest fielding shortstops in the game, great range, soft hands, with a career fielding average of .967. In 1945 he led all National League shortstops in assists, putouts, and double plays. In 1946 he made only 12 errors in 652 chances and led the league's shortstops with a fielding percentage of .982.

For some reason, Leo Durocher didn't like Kerr as a player, probably because he didn't produce much with the bat. Whatever the reason, soon after Leo became manager, he traded Kerr to the Braves. But that was the deal that brought us Alvin Dark and Eddie Stanky, so I guess you'd have to say the trade was justified.

When his playing career was over, Buddy settled in the New York area, living in New Jersey, and for many years he was a major league scout for the New York Mets.

Statistical Summaries

All statistics are for player's Giants career only.

HITTING

G = Games

H = Hits

HR = Home runs

RBI = Runs batted in

SB = Stolen bases

BA = Batting average

Shortstop	Years	G	H	HR	RBI	SB	BA
Travis Jackson *Had four extra-base hits (1 double, 1 triple, 2 home runs) on June 15, 1929*	1922–36	1,656	1,768	135	929	71	.291
Alvin Dark *Hit two doubles in one inning on September 14, 1952*	1950–56	933	1,106	98	429	41	.292
Dave Bancroft *Only Giant to play in every game in 1922*	1920–23, 1930	534	670	11	189	48	.310

continued	Years	G	H	HR	RBI	SB	BA
Dick Bartell *Batted .381 in 1936 World Series*	1935–38, 1941–43, 1946	835	858	60	293	35	.279
Buddy Kerr *Hit home run in first major league at-bat on September 8, 1943*	1943–49	843	756	28	269	38	.256

FIELDING

PO = Putouts

A = Assists

E = Errors

DP – Double plays

TC/G = Total chances divided by games played

FA = Fielding average

Shortstop	PO	A	E	DP	TC/G	FA
Travis Jackson	2,878	4,636	381	826	6.0	.952
Alvin Dark	1,717	2,639	187	612	5.1	.959
Dave Bancroft	1,316	1,966	185	319	6.7	.947
Dick Bartell	1,381	2,154	163	394	6.0	.956
Buddy Kerr	1,625	2,653	148	420	5.4	.967

63

FIVE

Third Baseman

Freddie Lindstrom was never considered more than an average fielder at third base and due to his defensive deficiencies and suffering from chronic back problems, he finished out his career in the outfield, but he's my choice as the number one third baseman in Giants history because of his bat and because he's the only Giant third baseman in the Hall of Fame.

Lindstrom joined the Giants in 1924 and made his major league debut at the age of 18 years, four months, and 24 days. He batted only .253 in 52 games, shuttling between third base and second base, but made his mark that fall, positively and negatively. He became the youngest ever to play in the World Series, appearing in all seven games and batting .333. In Game 5, he had four hits against the Washington Senators legendary "Big Train," Walter Johnson.

1. FREDDIE LINDSTROM

2. MATT WILLIAMS

3. SID GORDON

4. JIM DAVENPORT

5. JIM RAY HART

But Lindstrom became the unfortunate and unwitting Series goat. With the score tied, 3–3, in the bottom of the 12th of the seventh game, the Senators put runners on first and second with one out. Earl McNeely hit an easy roller to third and as Lindstrom was poised to field it and turn it into an

Freddie Lindstrom, as an old-timer in 1951, re-enacts his infamous play from the 1924 World Series, in which a ground ball hit a pebble (a sizable rock for this re-enactment) and bounded over his head to score the winning run in the twelfth inning of Game 7 against the Senators.

inning-ending double play, the ball took a wild, kangaroo hop over the Giants third baseman's head and Muddy Ruel scored all the way from second base with the Series-winning run.

Lindstrom recovered to take over third base for the Giants and bat a respectable .287 in 1925. He followed that up with six consecutive seasons batting over .300, including a .358 average and league-leading 231 hits in 1928 and a lusty .379 (teammate Bill Terry led the league with .401), 22 homers, and 106 RBIs in 1930, which would be Lindstrom's last season as a full-time third baseman.

Two years later, John McGraw retired as manager of the Giants and named Terry as his replacement. Lindstrom had assumed he would be McGraw's successor and when he was bypassed, he asked Terry to trade him. Terry obliged and sent Lindstrom to Pittsburgh the following season. It would be his final season as a regular.

After the 1934 season, he was traded to the Cubs and he helped them win the pennant in 1935 by batting .275 in 90 games filling in at third base and the outfield. On the move again, Lindstrom finished up his career with the Dodgers in 1936, but retired after playing in only 26 games.

After his retirement, Lindstrom managed three years in the minor leagues. Later, the native Chicagoan was head baseball coach at Northwestern University. He was elected to the Hall of Fame in 1976, five years before his death.

I saw **Matt Williams** when he first came to the Giants in 1987, and I remember thinking here was a young man who had a chance to be a special player. He was the strong, quiet type, a better-than-average fielder at third base who looked like he would be a strong hitter with great power.

What impressed me most about him was his work ethic, a tough kid who played hard and showed the desire to improve; what we call "a gamer."

What impressed me most about Matt Williams was his work ethic, a tough kid who played hard and showed the desire to improve; what we call "a gamer."

I'm pleased to say that I nailed that prediction pretty good, although it took a few years for Matt to get his feet solidly beneath him. He had trials with the Giants in 1987, 1988, and 1989, and while he showed occasional power, he didn't hit for much of an average. But when he took over the third base job in 1990, he really came on strong, belting 33 homers,

67

leading the National League with 122 RBIs, and raising his average to .277, a boost of 75 points over the previous season.

In the seven years from 1990 to 1996, Matt blasted 213 homers, drove in 642 runs, and improved his defense. His hard work paid off, and he won Gold Gloves in 1991, '93, and '94.

After the 1996 season, Williams was traded to the Cleveland Indians. The trade came a few days before Matt's 31st birthday and the Giants obviously figured his best days were behind him. It was a trade that didn't sit well with Giants fans. Matt was a popular player in San Francisco, and when he left, he was third in home runs and fourth in runs batted in among all the players on

Matt Williams, through his hard work and desire to improve, became a three-time Gold Glover at third base for the Giants.

the Giants team. Needless to say, he also had hit more home runs than any
Giants third baseman in history, San Francisco or New York.

But what general manager Brian Sabean did with that trade was turn
Williams into Jeff Kent, who hit 175 home runs and drove in 689 runs in his
six seasons in San Francisco. So, in 16 years, between Matt Williams and Jeff
Kent, the Giants got 422 home runs and 1,421 RBIs.

New York Giants fans were willing to forgive **Sid Gordon** for being born
and raised in Brooklyn once he settled in as their third baseman and began
to hit home runs, which he did in bunches.

The Giants had high hopes for Gordon. Not only was he a native New
Yorker, he was Jewish, and because New York City had a large Jewish pop-
ulation, all three New York teams were always on the lookout for a Jewish
star, but they never could find one.

The Yankees, Giants, and Dodgers all missed out on Hank Greenberg,
who was right under their noses, having been born and raised in the
Bronx.

The Yankees had Jimmy Reese, a substitute player of little note, and didn't
have a Jewish player of any consequence until Ron Blomberg in the 1970s.

The Dodgers had outfielders Goody Rosen and Cal Abrams, who were
marginal players. They finally landed a Jewish star when they signed Brooklyn native Sandy Koufax, but he didn't blossom into greatness until the
Dodgers had left Brooklyn.

The Giants had Andy Cohen, Harry Feldman, Harry Danning, and Phil
Weintraub, all of whom had mediocre careers, so you can clearly see why
they were hoping for big things from Gordon.

At the start of his career, Sid played all around the lot, mostly in the outfield.
After Freddie Lindstrom retired, the Giants searched high and low for another
third baseman with very little success. Third base was such a problem position
for them that in the 11 years from 1936 to 1947, they had 10 different players
get the bulk of the playing time there.

Gordon had produced fairly productive numbers in a utility role, playing
various positions. In an effort to get more production out of third base, considered a power position, they made Sid the third baseman in 1948, and he
responded with his best season, a .299 batting average, 30 home runs, and 107
RBIs. He followed that up the next year with a .284 average, 26 homers, and
90 runs batted in.

Sid Gordon was tough enough to knock down shots to third base with anything he could get in front of the ball. *Photo courtesy of Bettmann/CORBIS.*

Sid didn't run very well, but he could swing the bat and he made himself into a pretty good third baseman. He had a great arm and he was tough enough to knock down shots to third, off his arms, off his chest, and still throw the runner out.

When the Giants had a chance to land Alvin Dark and Eddie Stanky from the Braves, which would shore up their middle, Gordon had to be sacrificed. He went to Boston in the trade and had four good years with the Braves, including 56 homers and 212 RBIs his first two years in Boston.

After Sid Gordon left following the 1949 season, the Giants' search for a full-time, regular third baseman continued for almost a decade. And then, starting in 1958, two men held down the position for the next dozen years, and they're numbers four and five on my list of all-time Giants third basemen.

With their arrival in San Francisco, the Giants introduced a new third baseman, James Houston Davenport, out of Siluria, Alabama, and for the next six years, he gave the team consistency at third base they hadn't had since Freddie Lindstrom and defense they may never have had for any appreciable stretch of time.

*I*n his 15-year major league career, Bobby Thomson appeared in 1,779 games, only 184 of them as a third baseman.

But it was as a third baseman that he hit his famous home run, the greatest single on-field moment in baseball history, the three-run shot off Ralph Branca in the ninth inning of the third playoff game between the Giants and Dodgers in 1951, a home run that turned a 4–2 Dodgers lead into a 5–4 Giants victory and won the National League pennant.

Thomson's blow, the "shot heard 'round the world," climaxed a comeback from a 13½ game deficit to the Dodgers in August and a game-winning, pennant-winning four-run rally by the Giants in that decisive playoff game—a rally started when Alvin Dark led off the bottom of the ninth by slapping a single past Dodgers first baseman Gil Hodges into right field.

As field leader, captain, and shortstop of the Giants, Dark played alongside Thomson in the Giants infield and marveled at how the tall Scotsman adapted to a position he hadn't played in five years.

By mid-May in the 1951 season, with the Giants struggling to reach the .500 level, word circulated around the team that they were bringing up 20-year-old Willie Mays from Minneapolis to play center field, a move Dark was slow to embrace.

"I went to Herman Franks (a Giants coach) and said, 'What are we doing bringing up a center fielder? We've already got the best center fielder in the National League.'

"I always prefaced my remarks by saying when you're playing in the Polo Grounds, with its spacious center field, you better have a guy who can run and go get the ball, and nobody could do that better than Bobby. But I guess it worked out all right," Dark said with a laugh.

The reason it worked out all right, according to Dark, was not only the brilliance of Mays, but also the ability of Thomson to make the switch seamlessly:

For a guy who had been playing center field, it took a lot of guts to move to third base. My goodness, it would be like me switching from shortstop to center field. I couldn't do it. Bobby made it look easy, and it wasn't.

I'm not saying he was as good as Red Rolfe, but he played a very good third base. Most outfielders, the first thing they do when they move to the infield is get out of the way of hot line drives. Not Bobby. One thing I noticed right away was that when there was a runner on first base and there was a ground ball hit to him, he was already stepping toward second base to start the double play. You can tell when a guy does that that he's a pretty good athlete. Bobby Thomson was a very good athlete.

As a hitter, he was one of the best I've ever seen in the clutch, and not just because of that one home run. I can't tell you how many games he won for us that season with home runs. A lot of people forget that in the first game of that playoff in Brooklyn, we were losing, 1–0, and Bobby hit a two-run homer off Branca in the fourth inning and we won the game, 3–1.

The last time I saw Bobby, we got together when he came down to South Carolina for an appearance a few years ago. He told me he couldn't believe that so many years later, he was still being asked to make appearances. "Can you imagine," he said, "I hit one home run and people still remember."

That's Bobby Thomson. And that's why he has always been one of my favorite people.

Jim Davenport made an immediate impression on Giants manager Bill Rigney, my old teammate, who was one of those 10 third basemen in 11 years I spoke about earlier. Rigney called Davenport, "The greatest third baseman I ever saw; at least the only one I'd compare to Billy Cox [the Dodgers magician at third base in the '50s]."

As a hitter, Davenport was consistently around .250 to .260, but without much power. His high for home runs in a season was 14 in 1962. But with Willie Mays, Willie McCovey, Orlando Cepeda, Felipe Alou, Ed Bailey, and Tom Haller, the Giants had enough bats. What they needed from Davenport was defense, and they got it. He led National League third basemen in fielding three times, won a Gold Glove in 1962, and once, during the 1967 season, played 65 consecutive errorless games at third.

In 1964 a young power hitter named Jim Ray Hart, number five on my all-time list of Giants third basemen, came along, and manager Al Dark handed him the third-base job. Davenport showed his versatility by playing all three infield positions and some in the outfield. When Hart injured his right shoulder and could hardly throw the ball across the diamond, Davenport again became the Giants' primary third baseman for two more seasons.

Davenport played his entire 13-year major league career as a San Francisco Giant and when he retired in 1970, he became a coach for the Giants, a job he held until 1985 when, after 26 years in the uniform of the San Francisco Giants, he was named manager of the team.

But on September 19, with his team 32 games under .500 and in sixth place (last in the National League West), he quit the job and was replaced by Roger Craig.

Jim Davenport (left), shown with the Yankees' Clete Boyer prior to a World Series game in 1962, gave the Giants defense at third base, the likes of which they hadn't seen in a long time. *Photo courtesy of Diamond Images/Getty Images.*

Had he been able to avoid injury, or adapt to playing third base, **Jim Ray Hart** could have been one of the greatest players in Giants history. Or if he came along a few years later and played in the American League, with the designated hitter, he might have been regarded as one of the great hitters of his era.

As it was, Hart put up tremendous numbers in his first five full seasons as a Giant, from 1964 to 1968, averaging almost 90 RBIs and 28 home runs per season and batting .285 or better four times.

Unfortunately, Jim was injury-prone. In fact, in one of his first major league games, Bob Gibson plunked him in the back with a fastball and broke

Jim Ray Hart had the potential and ability to go down as one of the greatest Giants of all time and would have had he not had some unfortuate injuries. *Photo courtesy of Bettmann/CORBIS.*

his shoulder blade. A few days after he got back, Curt Simmons hit him in the head and put Hart out for the rest of the season.

He came back in 1964 to hit 31 home runs, a rookie record for the San Francisco Giants. In one game, he not only hit for the cycle, he tied a major league record by driving in six runs in one inning.

In 1969, Hart suffered a serious injury to his right shoulder and his career spiraled downward thereafter. In his final six seasons with the Giants and the Yankees (where he finally got to be a DH), he appeared in only 355 games and hit only 31 home runs.

Once he hurt his shoulder, Jim's career as a third baseman was over, although he never was known for his defense, mainly because he hated playing the position.

Jim never spoke much. He was a guy who chewed toothpicks at bat and in the field and seemed to always have a smile on his face, but rarely spoke. Except when someone asked him about playing third base. Then he said a mouthful. Third base, he said, is "just too damn close to the hitters."

As a guy who played a lot of third base, I second the motion.

Statistical Summaries

All statistics are for player's Giants career only.

HITTING

G = Games
H = Hits
HR = Home runs
RBI = Runs batted in
SB = Stolen bases
BA = Batting average

Third Baseman	Years	G	H	HR	RBI	SB	BA
Freddie Lindstrom *His 231 hits in 1928 led the league*	1924–32	1,087	1,347	91	603	80	.318
Matt Williams *Drove in nine runs in five-game NLCS against Chicago in 1989*	1987–96	1,120	1,092	247	732	29	.264
Sid Gordon *Slammed two home runs in one inning on July 31, 1949*	1941–43, 1946–49, 1955	760	714	90	393	14	.278

continued	Years	G	H	HR	RBI	SB	BA
Jim Davenport *Hit a pinch-hit grand slam against Cincinnati on July 8, 1966*	1958–70	1,501	1,142	77	456	16	.258
Jim Ray Hart *Drove in six runs in one inning on July 8, 1970*	1963–73	1,001	965	157	526	17	.282

FIELDING

PO = Putouts

A = Assists

E = Errors

DP = Double plays

TC/G = Total chances divided by games played

FA = Fielding average

Third Baseman	PO	A	E	DP	TC/G	FA
Freddie Lindstrom	804	1,501	98	128	3.1	.959
Matt Williams	807	1,976	118	198	2.9	.959
Sid Gordon	341	665	54	58	2.9	.949
Jim Davenport	863	1,816	100	155	2.5	.964
Jim Ray Hart	564	1,187	134	92	2.8	.929

SIX

Left Fielder

I don't know **Barry Bonds**, never met the man, but what little I know about him from what I have read, I'm not a Barry Bonds fan. He seems to me to be surly and self-absorbed, not at all like his father, and there are the rumors and innuendoes of his possible drug use.

I don't know anything about that. I'm not a detective or an investigator. I'm not the steroid police. I've heard the allegations, but as this is written, there has been no admission on his part, no action taken against him, no charges, no penalty. Until there is any of that, I'll leave it to the baseball administrators and historians to determine if Bonds's accomplishments were chemically aided. Meanwhile, in this country a man is innocent until he's proven guilty, so until Bonds is proven guilty of using steroids, I can only go

1. BARRY BONDS

2. MONTE IRVIN

3. JOE "JO-JO" MOORE

4. IRISH MEUSEL

5. KEVIN MITCHELL

by his record and his record cannot be ignored. It emphatically says he is the greatest left fielder in Giants history and, along with Willie Mays and Mel Ott, one of the three greatest players the Giants ever had.

Just look at his 2001 season, maybe the greatest single season for a slugger in baseball history, and that includes Babe Ruth, Henry Aaron, and Bonds's

Barry Bonds's numbers are simply staggering, and he rates not only as the Giants' top left fielder but also as one of the three best players the franchise has ever had.

godfather, Willie Mays. In that 2001 season, Bonds batted .328, drove in 137 runs, stole 13 bases in 16 attempts, scored 129 runs, had a slugging percentage of .863 (a major league record), had an on-base percentage of .515, and hit a major league record 73 home runs in only 476 official at-bats. That's one home run for every 6.52 at-bats. Phenomenal!

He also drew 177 walks, of which 35 of them were intentional.

And it doesn't stop there.

In 2002, he batted .370, hit 46 home runs, scored 117 runs, drove in 110, had a slugging percentage of .799 and an on-base percentage of .582, and drew 198 walks, 68 of them intentional.

In 2003, he batted .341, hit 45 homers, scored 111 runs, drove in 90, had a slugging percentage of .749 and an on-base percentage of .529, and drew 148 walks, 61 of them intentional.

And in 2004, he batted .362, again hit 45 homers, scored 129 runs, drove in 101, had a slugging percentage of .812 and an on-base percentage of .609 (a major league record), and drew the unbelievable record total of 232 walks, of which 120 were intentional, also a record. That's more intentional walks than Aaron ever received in one season, intentional and unintentional combined. The most walks Ruth ever received in one season (there is no record of Ruth's intentional walks) was 170, so in 2004, Bonds drew 52 more walks than Ruth did in his best season for walks.

The numbers are simply staggering, and his accomplishments took up 20 pages in the Giants 2005 media guide.

Here are only some of Bonds's accomplishments through the 2005 season:

- Seven Most Valuable Player awards, a record
- Third player to hit 700 home runs for his career, joining Henry Aaron and Babe Ruth
- Eight Gold Gloves
- The major league single-season record holder in home runs, walks, intentional walks, on-base percentage, slugging percentage, home-run ratio, and home-run percentage
- The all-time leader in walks and intentional walks
- The first member of the 500/500 club, 500 homers and 500 stolen bases
- A major league record 13 consecutive 30-home-run seasons

- A National League record 12 100-RBI seasons
- A National League record 12 100-walk seasons
- Eight seasons with 40 or more home runs, tying Aaron's National League record
- Six seasons with 30 homers and 30 stolen bases

What more can I say?

I said it before, and I'll say it again, the guy responsible more than anybody for our comeback in 1951, for getting us to wipe out the Dodgers 13½ game lead and forcing a playoff, was **Monte Irvin.** Without Monte, there would have been no playoff. He was our big guy. It was Monte who carried us on his back most of the times in the second half of the season.

Monte Irvin was an exceptional talent and an even better human being. I had as much respect for him as for anybody I've ever played with.

I had as much respect for Monte as anybody I ever played with, as a player and as a man. I was impressed with him from the first time I saw him. His physique! He was built like a panther. Strong. All muscle. He could run, he could hit, and hit for power. He could do everything. We all respected him. Anybody who knew him respected him. He was a quiet, nice guy, soft-spoken and polite: a true gentleman.

What a season he had in 1951, one of the best ever when it came to getting big hits, game-winning hits. He batted .312, hit 24 home runs and 121 RBIs, and then he batted .458 in the World Series against the Yankees and stole home against Allie Reynolds in the first game.

After that season, I enjoyed going out on speaking engagements with Monte because I liked his company and because it gave me a chance to give him the recognition he deserved. I got a lot of pleasure out of saying, "Yeah, I'm the guy that hit the home run, but without this guy we wouldn't have been there at the end." And I meant it. He was the reason we had a chance to beat the Dodgers.

Irvin should have been the Most Valuable Player that year, but he finished third, behind Roy Campanella and Stan Musial, who hit for higher averages and more home runs. But Monte led the league in RBIs, and it seemed that most of them either won a game for us or gave us a lead.

If there was a big surprise in the ninth inning of that third playoff game against the Dodgers, it was that Irvin popped out with two on and none out.

Irvin remembers that game:

When I really wanted to get a base hit, I usually tried to go to right field, and that was my thinking in that at-bat. My main thought was that I didn't want to hit into a double play and kill the rally. So I tried to go to right field and Newcombe threw me a slider and I popped it up in foul territory off first base. There was a lot of room in foul territory in the Polo Grounds and Gil Hodges went over, reached into the seats, and caught the damn ball.

I thought Newcombe was still throwing pretty good in that ninth inning. Leo Durocher always said if he had been the manager of the Dodgers, he wouldn't have taken Newcombe out. Or if he did take him out, he would have brought in either Carl Erskine or Clem Labine throwing that sinker like he did the day before when he shut us out. Labine could have faced one or two hitters; it wouldn't have hurt him.

The break we got was Erskine being a little wild and the ball getting away in the bullpen. Otherwise they would have brought him in instead of Branca and who knows how that would have turned out? Ralph was throwing great; his problem with Thomson was just bad location.

We also got a break because Roy Campanella was hurt and wasn't catching that day. After Branca threw that first strike to Thomson, a fast ball up and in, right in his wheelhouse—we almost fell off the bench when Bobby took that first pitch; luckily, he didn't take the second one—Campy would have gone out and told him, "We've got to keep the ball down and away. This guy's a pull hitter and if he hits one of those sliders down and away, more power to him. But let's not help him."

I once asked Ralph what his thinking was against Thomson and he said he wanted to throw him the same pitch as the first one to set him up and then they were going to work on him. But he was one pitch too late and he made it too good.

Horace Stoneham, the Giants owner, and Sal Maglie, who started the game for us, didn't even see Thomson's home run. In the bottom of the ninth inning, they headed for the clubhouse. They walked underneath the stands, all the way around the stadium to the clubhouse.

Photographers had set up their cameras anticipating a pennant-clinching celebration in the Dodgers clubhouse. Newcombe was in the shower when Thomson hit his homer and when he came out of the shower he saw the photographers starting to break down their cameras.

"What are you guys doing?" Newcombe asked them.

"The Giants win the pennant," they said.

"Bull" said Newcombe.

"Hey, Newk," they said, "the Giants win the pennant."

Newcombe couldn't believe it, and neither could thousands of other people.

We all expected Monte to get a base hit in that spot, because he had done it all year long, but I guess it just wasn't his time. Just as it wasn't his time when Branch Rickey chose Jackie Robinson to be the first black player in organized baseball in 1946. It could easily have been Monte. He had the right temperament, the right demeanor, and the right lifestyle to have been the guy. They were the same age—Jackie was 25 days older than Monte—and people who followed the Negro Leagues have said that Irvin was a better player than Robinson.

Rickey actually contacted Irvin and sounded him out about signing with the Dodgers (can you imagine a Dodgers outfield with Irvin in left, Duke Snider in center, and Carl Furillo in right?), but Monte had just returned from three years in the army and felt he had to play himself in shape before taking that big a step. He wanted to be ready when his time came.

What if Irvin had signed with the Dodgers? Would he have been the first black man in organized baseball? I don't know. What we do know is that Rickey chose Robinson. Why? Maybe it was because Robinson was ready and Irvin wasn't. Maybe it was because Rickey didn't want to pay the Newark Eagles, Monte's Negro League team, for the rights to his contract. Maybe it was because Robinson had been a big three-sport star at UCLA, or that Jackie had been a second lieutenant in the army. Or maybe it was because Jackie was more outspoken, more of a fighter, and had a chip on his shoulder and Monte was more laid back.

Whatever the reason, Robinson made history and it all worked out for the good, for baseball and certainly for the Giants.

Monte signed with the Giants in 1949 and was sent to Jersey City in the International League. By July, he was batting .373, so the Giants brought him to New York. He was 30 years old by then, and many of his most productive years were behind him. That's the tragedy of it all, that so many African Americans, like Irvin, didn't get their chance in the major leagues until they were older and many of their best days were behind them.

Soon after Irvin and Henry Thompson joined us, we took a trip to Chicago. I remember getting off the train and climbing aboard the bus to take us to our hotel, all of us except Irvin and Thompson. They got off the train and had to wait for a cab to take them to the Negro section of town. I was sitting on the bus next to Davey Williams and I remember saying to Davey, "It's not right. Why can't these guys come and stay with us? They're on our team."

Years later, after baseball, I made a trip with Monte to Canada, and they gave him a hard time going through customs. That really ticked him off. It was the only time in all the years I've known him that I ever saw Irvin angry.

Once Irvin got to the Giants, he made the most of the time he had. In 1950, his first full season, he batted .299, and then he had his big season in '51. He was at the top of his game, but the next year, he broke his ankle. He came back in 1953 and had another big year, a .329 average, 21 homers, and 97 RBIs, but he would never be the same again. He was getting older and the problem with his ankle had slowed him.

After he retired, Irvin scouted for the Mets for a few years, and then Bowie Kuhn brought him into the commissioner's office as a public relations ambassador for baseball. In 1973, the Committee on Negro Baseball Leagues elected Irvin to the Hall of Fame.

Every championship team needs a capable leadoff batter and the Giants' National League pennant winners of 1933, 1936, and 1937, had a good one in left fielder **Joe "Jo-Jo" Moore,** a left-handed slap hitter who played his entire 12-year career with the Giants, batted over .300 five times, and had a lifetime batting average of .298.

Moore was atypical of a leadoff batter in that he was a notorious first ball hitter who drew more than 40 walks in a season only four times. Because of his penchant for swinging at the first pitch, some managers insisted that their pitchers throw their first delivery to Moore out of the strike zone and fined any pitcher who allowed him to get a first pitch hit. As a result, some pitchers fired their first pitch at Moore's head, which angered Moore's roommate, 6'2", 205-pound muscleman Hank Leiber, who once told Dizzy Dean to stop throwing at Moore's head or he'd break every bone in the Cardinals ace's body.

Moore twice had more than 200 hits in a season and in three consecutive years, 1934–36, he scored more than 100 runs.

In the 1937 World Series against the Yankees, Moore tied a record for a five-game Series with nine hits and batted .391, tops for the Giants and better than Joe DiMaggio, Lou Gehrig, and Bill Dickey.

Joe Moore (second from left) and teammate Mel Ott clown around with Joe DiMaggio (second from right) and Lou Gehrig of the Yankees before the start of the 1937 World Series. *Photo courtesy of Bettmann/CORBIS.*

Irish Meusel batted over .300 four of his five seasons in New York and never below .292. *Photo courtesy of Bettmann/CORBIS.*

Irish Meusel, whose real first name was Emil, wasn't Irish. He got his nick-name because he looked like an Irishman, and he gets a place on my all-time Giants team because of five and a half outstanding seasons in New York, from midway in 1921 to 1926, when he batted over .300 four times and never lower than .292.

Meusel was a mediocre outfielder for the Phillies with a reputation for being lackadaisical when the Giants got him in July of 1921 for three players and $30,000. Irish suddenly gained motivation playing under the fiery Giants manager John McGraw, who seemed to impose his will on Meusel. McGraw made him his cleanup batter and Irish, who hustled as he never had in Philadelphia, responded with four consecutive 100 RBI seasons from 1922–25, including a personal high of 132 in 1922 and a league-leading 125 in 1923.

Irish was the older brother of Bob Meusel, the strapping, muscular, power-hitting outfielder of the Yankees' famed "Murderers Row" of the 1920s, but to look at them, you'd never take them for brothers. Bob Meusel was a giant of a man at 6'3", 190 pounds who won the American League home-run title in 1925, one of only two times in a 10-year stretch from 1920 to 1929 that Babe Ruth did not win it. Irish Meusel was some four inches shorter and 12 pounds lighter than his "little" brother, but he led the Giants in home runs in 1923 and 1925, and helped them win four consecutive National League championships from 1921–24.

In the first three of those pennant years, the Giants faced the Yankees in the World Series, so it was brother vs. brother. And big brother had the upper hand. His Giants won the World Series in '21, five games to three, with Irish out-hitting Bob .345 to .200, and in '22, in a four-game sweep, with Irish hitting the Giants' only home run and Bob hitting none. In the 1923 Series, Irish batted .280 with a home run and three RBIs. Bob hit .269, again failed to hit a home run, but drove in eight runs and the Yankees won their first World Series, four games to two.

After slipping to a .292 average, his lowest as a Giant, hitting only six home runs and driving in 65 runs in 1926, Irish was released by the Giants. He hooked on with the Dodgers, batted only .243 in 42 games, mostly as a pinch-hitter, and retired.

If **Kevin Mitchell** played his entire career the way he played for the Giants in 1989 and 1990, he would have been a perennial all-star and might have made the Hall of Fame.

Mitchell had come to the Giants in July of 1987 in a trade with San Diego, his major league career never living up to his potential. He had played all around the lot. In 1986, his rookie season with the Mets, he played six different positions, including 24 games at shortstop, which made for a rare sight—the 5'11", muscular 210-pound Mitchell at shortstop.

If Kevin Mitchell played his entire career the way he played for the Giants in 1989 and 1990, he would have been a perennial all-star and might have made the Hall of Fame.

In 1989, the Giants made Mitchell their left fielder. He put on contact lenses and started being tutored by batting coach Dusty Baker. The change was amazing. That year, Mitchell raised his average 40 points, to .291, led the National League in home runs with 47 and RBIs with 125, and was named the league's Most Valuable Player.

$\mathscr{A}$ trio of former New York Mets was sitting around at Shea Stadium one day, reminiscing about the good old days, when someone mentioned Kevin Mitchell, and the name immediately produced a flood of memories from Rusty Staub, Keith Hernandez, and Ron Darling.

The year was 1986, and Staub, coping with life as a retired player after an extremely lengthy and distinguished 23-year major league career (2,716 hits, 292 home runs, 1,466 RBIs) had been invited to spend spring training with the Mets. He recalled:

> *Frank Cashen (Mets general manager at the time) wanted me to help with the young players and one of them was Kevin Mitchell. I knew he had a world of talent. I had seen him two years before when the Mets brought him up for a few games at the end of the season, but this was going to be his rookie year. The first thing I did was make him get all his old stuff out of his locker and made sure he got all new equipment, bats, gloves, batting gloves, the works; kind of a fresh start.*
>
> *I grew to care a great deal about Kevin. It was one of those things that when you try to help someone, you get close and you find yourself pulling for him to do well. It wasn't that we became exceptionally good friends, but I tried to give him things to think about: to have an idea when he went to the plate. I talked to him about knowing what the pitcher was trying to do to get him out. I preached to him that a lot of times, in the clutch, if you're a guy who can hit, you have to go against the grain. If you're looking for a fastball down the middle, you're not going to see one, so you have to be prepared for something else. To watch how he progressed in 1986 and then went on to do all the wonderful things he did in his career was very rewarding for me. He could hit. He could flat hit.*

"Whenever people ask me to describe the 1986 team, which I think is impossible, all I can come up with is that Kevin Mitchell was our utility player," said Ron Darling. "That's how good that team was. Kevin played six positions that season [he batted .277, hit 12 home runs, and drove in 43 runs in 328 at-bats]."

Keith Hernandez remembered Mitchell's enormous contribution in the sixth game of the '86 World Series against the Red Sox, the Mookie Wilson–Bill Buckner game. The Red Sox, up three games to two, broke a 3–3 tie with two runs in the top of the 10th. When Wally Backman flied to left and Hernandez flied to center, the Sox were one out away from their first World Series victory in 68 years, and the person in charge of putting messages on the Shea Stadium scoreboard jumped the gun and flashed "Congratulations to the World Champions Boston Red Sox."

But Gary Carter kept the Mets' flickering hopes alive by lining a single to left.

"I was in the clubhouse, taking off my uniform," Hernandez said. "Mitchell was in the clubhouse, too. People said he wasn't dressed, but that's not true. He was dressed. He was sitting in front of his locker and (coach) Buddy Harrelson had to come and get him (to pinch-hit for pitcher Rick Aguilera).

"'Get your butt out here,' Buddy said."

"Calvin Schiraldi threw him a cutter," Darling recalled, "and he hit it off the end of the bat and blooped it into left center."

It was a clutch hit for the rookie, one of the biggest hits of that magical season. Ray Knight followed with another bloop hit to score Carter and send Mitchell to third. Bob Stanley replaced Schiraldi and uncorked a wild pitch allowing Mitchell to score the tying run and Knight to go to second. Buckner then flubbed Wilson's easiest of slow rollers and Knight scored the winning run. In Game 7, the Mets would rally from three runs down and win, 8–5, once again denying the Red Sox of a world championship.

That winter, Mitchell was traded to San Diego.

"There were a lot of ramifications to that because San Diego was his home and he was being taken advantage of by his brother and his old friends," said Staub. "The Padres traded him to San Francisco and the change, getting away from his old environment, did wonders for him. Kevin just blossomed in San Francisco like you never saw. He was Most Valuable Player (in 1989) and he deserved it."

"He changed his stance just a little bit," said Darling. "He moved closer to the plate and you couldn't get in on him."

Kevin Mitchell had two monster years in left field for the Giants, including his MVP season of 1989. *Photo courtesy of Getty Images.*

"Kevin was an adventure in the field every once in awhile," said Staub, "but he did a good job and the versatility of his time with the Mets, especially, was outstanding. He came into his own in San Francisco. He hit the tough pitchers and he was a force to contend with. He was so strong. People don't realize how strong he was."

Mitchell followed that up with a .290 average, 35 homers, and 93 RBIs in 1990, but never reached those heights again and was traded to Seattle after the 1991 season.

Defensively, Mitchell was not your idea of a smooth operator at any position, but he had good hands, and he did have his moments, one in particular. Early in the 1989 season, a ball was hit to left field over his head. Mitchell went back for it and overran the ball. In desperation, he reached back and caught the ball in his bare hand.

Statistical Summaries

All statistics are for player's Giants career only.

HITTING

G = Games

H = Hits

HR = Home runs

RBI = Runs batted in

SB = Stolen bases

BA = Batting average

Left Fielder	Years	G	H	HR	RBI	SB	BA
Barry Bonds *Set World Series record in 2002 by drawing 13 walks*	1993–2006	1,720	1,758	532	1,297	255	.316
Monte Irvin *One of five Giants to hit 20 or more home runs (21) in 1953*	1949–55	653	639	84	393	27	.296
Joe "Jo-Jo" Moore *Tough to double up, hit into only 48 DP in over 5000 at-bats*	1930–41	1,335	1,615	79	513	46	.298

continued	Years	G	H	HR	RBI	SB	BA
Irish Meusel *Reached double figures in doubles (28), triples (17), home runs (16), and steals (12) in 1922*	1921–26	765	931	70	571	46	.314
Kevin Mitchell *In 1989, 87 of his 158 hits (55 percent) went for extra bases*	1987–91	624	614	143	411	23	.278

FIELDING

PO = Putouts

A = Assists

E = Errors

DP = Double plays

TC/G = Total chances divided by games played

FA = Fielding average

Left Fielder	PO	A	E	DP	TC/G	FA
Barry Bonds	3,160	97	56	16	1.9	.983
Monte Irvin	1,017	39	20	6	2.2	.981
Joe "Jo-Jo" Moore	2,501	116	68	17	2.1	.975
Irish Meusel	1,397	65	55	6	2.1	.964
Kevin Mitchell	845	25	28	4	2.1	.969

SEVEN

Center Fielder

Willie Mays was born to play baseball, and he played it with verve and zest and a boyish enthusiasm that infected all those around him. He also played it as well as anybody I've ever seen.

When the 1951 season started, I was in center field for the Giants, and we kept hearing about this kid phenom from Alabama, who had been playing in the Negro Leagues since he was 17 and who had been signed by the Giants the previous year. He had a super season in Trenton, and now he was tearing up the American Association with Minneapolis, the Giants' top farm team.

1. WILLIE MAYS

2. CHILI DAVIS

3. HANK LEIBER

4. BENNY KAUFF

5. GARRY MADDOX

By the middle of May, Mays was hitting .477 at Minneapolis and Durocher kept asking the Giants to bring him up. Naturally, I was wondering what was to become of me, but I got an inkling when Durocher, who knew I had played the infield, had me go to third base during practice. He hit me ground balls, to my left, to my right, and I bounced around pretty good. After awhile, Durocher said, "I've seen enough. He can play."

Willie Mays struggled with the bat when he first came up to the Giants as a 20-year-old, but he was making great plays in center field from the very start.

I hadn't played the infield since 1947, when I played nine games at second base, and I hadn't played third base since 1946, when I played there for the Giants in 16 games. But if Durocher wanted me to play third base, and it would help the ballclub, I was willing to do it.

I was never a pop-off guy. I was brought up to take things as they are and not complain. We never had that much at home. My mother had a saying, "Be thankful for small mercies." That's the way I was brought up. If Leo wanted me to go to third base, I'd go there without a word, even though I thought I was doing a pretty good job in center field.

Willie Mays was born to play baseball, and he played it with verve and zest and a boyish enthusiasm that infected all those around him.

So the Giants brought Mays up on May 25, 19 days after his 20th birthday, stuck him in center field, and put me at third base.

Things didn't go well for Willie at first. He went hitless in his first 12 at-bats and got his first hit in the Polo Grounds on May 28, a home run against the Boston Braves off Warren Spahn, who would win 22 games that season and finish his career with 363 wins, the most ever by a left-hander. It was our only run in a 4–1 defeat to the Braves. After that hit, Mays went into another slump, 12 more at-bats without a hit, and he began to have some self-doubts.

As the story goes, Mays went to Durocher in tears. He supposedly said, "Mr. Leo, I can't do it. I'm not good enough to play here."

And Leo is said to have told him, "Willie, if you don't get another hit all year, you're still my center fielder, so relax and don't worry about being sent back to the minor leagues. All I want you to do is catch everything they hit your way."

It was completely out of character for Durocher. Leo was never known to take that sort of gentle approach with young players. Why did he do it this time? Either it was because he saw something in Willie that others might not have seen, or it was an ego thing with Durocher. He had pushed hard to bring Mays up and he didn't want to be proved wrong. Willie was Leo's baby and he was going to give him every chance to make it.

Durocher got a lot of credit for his handling of Mays, babying him and bringing him along, and deservedly so. But when the game was over, Durocher went his way and Willie went his way, and it was Monte Irvin who really took Willie under his wing, like a big brother, an uncle, or a surrogate father.

Who was baseball's greatest player? Was it Babe Ruth or Ty Cobb? Honus Wagner or "Shoeless" Joe Jackson?

Was it Joe DiMaggio, who in the last decades of his life was always introduced as "Baseball's greatest living player"?

Was it Henry Aaron, the reigning home run king, or is it Barry Bonds, the home run king-in-waiting? Or do we eliminate Bonds because of the suspicion that his achievements were chemically aided?

Or is baseball's greatest player none of the above? Is it Willie Mays, who played the game with such flair, such joy, such childish enthusiasm, and such skill?

The debate rages on. There is no wrong answer, merely a matter of opinion.

But one thing is certain: no debate of baseball's greatest player is complete without the mention of Willie Mays. Here, then, is how Mays is viewed by his peers, his contemporaries, and by Mays himself.

Ted Williams: "When you say Willie Mays, you gotta think of DiMaggio, and when you say DiMaggio, you gotta think of Willie Mays. They were two super, super players."

Fresco Thompson (Dodgers executive): "Willie Mays and his glove—where triples go to die."

Monte Irvin: "It was his solemn duty to catch any ball that wasn't in the stands."

Bill Rigney: "As a batter, his only weakness is a wild pitch."

Warren Spahn: "He was something like 0-for-20 (actually 0-for-12) the first time I saw him. His first major league hit was a home run off me and I'll never forgive myself. We might have gotten rid of Willie forever if I'd only struck him out."

Peter Magowan (San Francisco Giants president): "He would routinely do things you never saw anyone else do. He'd score from first base on a single. He'd take two bases on a pop-up. He'd throw somebody out at the plate on one bounce. And the bigger the game, the better he played."

Sandy Koufax: "I can't believe that Babe Ruth was a better player than Willie Mays. Ruth is to baseball what Arnold Palmer is to golf. He got the game moving. But I can't believe he could run as well as Mays, and I can't believe he was any better an outfielder."

Gil Hodges (New York Mets manager): "I can't very well tell my batters don't hit it to him. Wherever they hit it, he's there anyway."

Gaylord Perry: "He always waited until the last second to commit himself and that's why he was so good at hitting the breaking ball. He could pick up the spin on the ball, and he always had his hands in the right position to adjust."

Red Smith: "Duke Snider, Mickey Mantle, and Willie Mays. You could get a fat lip in any saloon by starting an argument as to which was best. One point was beyond argument, though. Willie was by all odds the most exciting."

San Francisco sportswriter **Bob Stevens** (after Mays hit a wicked line shot in the outfield gap): "The only man who could catch that ball just hit it."

Mickey Mantle: "They used to argue, who was better, Mays, Snider, or me. There is no argument. Just look at the record. Willie was the best."

Ted Kluszewski: "I'm not sure what the hell charisma is, but I get the feeling it's Willie Mays."

Charlie Dressen (after Mays had a spectacular catch against his Dodgers): "I'd like to see him do it again."

Reggie Jackson: "I used to dream how good it would be to be Mickey Mantle or Willie Mays. My dreams have died."

Reggie Jackson (again): "You used to think if the score was 5–0, he'd hit a five-run homer."

Leo Durocher: "I never saw a [bleeping] ball go out of a [bleeping] ballpark so [bleeping] fast in my [bleeping] life."

Leo Durocher (again, describing Mays): "Joe Louis, Jascha Heifetz, Sammy Davis, and Nashua rolled into one."

Leo Durocher (once more): "If he could cook I'd marry him."

Willie Mays on Willie Mays: "I can't tell you about moments because I wasn't into that. I just played every day and enjoyed what I was doing. When I made a great catch it was just routine. I didn't worry about it. Winning was important. Winning."

"I didn't think like that (about best seasons). What if you thought 1997 was your best year, what would you do now? I never looked back. I couldn't dwell on last year's season. I always looked forward. I never worried about what other people were doing—except the guy I was playing against."

(Asked which was his greatest catch): "I don't compare 'em, I just catch 'em."

(On Joe DiMaggio insisting he be introduced as the greatest living ballplayer): "I don't know what Joe wanted, but I don't have a problem if he wanted to do that. He was my hero. Joe was the best all-around player. Joe was the best."

"If you can run, hit, run the bases, hit with power, field, throw, and do all other things that are part of the game, then you're a good ballplayer."

"A lot of people said when I was 40, I should quit, but I don't think so. You should play as long as you can and as long as you enjoy the game. In 1973, I wasn't enjoying the game, so I quit in May, I retired, and they wouldn't let me retire. So I finished up in the World Series. But I say to players, 'Play as long as you can because you only have one chance.'"

"When I'm not hitting, I don't hit nobody. But when I'm hitting, I hit anybody."

"They throw the ball, I hit it. They hit the ball, I catch it."

"I think I was the best baseball player I ever saw."

Once Mays was assured his job was safe, he relaxed and began to play the way Durocher thought he would. After his slow start, Willie ended up contributing a lot. He finished the season batting a respectable .274, with 20 home runs and 68 RBIs, and he was voted National League Rookie of the Year. And he was the answer to what became a popular baseball trivia question.

"Who was on deck when Bobby Thomson hit the home run that beat the Dodgers in the third game of the 1951 National League playoff?"

Mays was on deck, and later he told me, "I'm glad you hit that home run; it took the pressure off me."

Once he started to play better, Mays was fun to be around. He had this high-pitched voice and was very talkative, not a shy little kid. He'd get into these pepper games and he was so animated, people flocked around him and kidded with him. The writers and the fans loved him. He was a joy for photographers who would go up to Harlem and take pictures of Willie playing stickball in the street with a bunch of neighborhood kids.

Despite his early struggles with the bat, Willie brought his glove with him from the start. He made some plays right away and he had a terrific arm and that's what Durocher saw that made him stick with Mays.

Willie played with a flair. His cap would come flying off when he raced after a fly ball, and he'd make those basket catches. He was part showman and all ballplayer. He made plays in the outfield you just couldn't believe.

Everybody talks about his catch in the Polo Grounds in the first game of the 1954 World Series. It was the top of the eighth inning with the score tied, 2–2. The Indians had runners on first and second with no outs when Vic Wertz sent a tremendous drive to the deepest part of center field. At the crack of the bat, Mays turned and with his back to home plate, raced to the wall, glanced up, and caught the ball over his shoulder, 430 feet away from home plate. Then he whirled and threw the ball back into the infield.

What made that catch so memorable was that it came in a World Series game with millions watching on television, and it came with the game on the line. The catch killed a rally and stopped Cleveland dead in its tracks. The Giants won that game on Dusty Rhodes's pinch-hit three-run home run in the bottom of the tenth, and went on to sweep the Indians in four games.

But even Mays said that wasn't the best catch he ever made.

The one I remember was against the Dodgers in the Polo Grounds. There was a runner at third and Carl Furillo hit a drive to right center and Willie raced over and just got his glove on it on the full run, and then in one motion, he turned and threw a strike to home plate to get the runner attempting to tag up and score from third. You never do that. You just don't make plays like that. Just think, you're on a full run, you make the catch, and then you spin around and throw a strike to home plate, more than 300 feet away. That ball has to be released at just the right moment. Willie may be the only player who ever lived who could have made a play like that.

After the catch, Dodgers manager Charlie Dressen said, "I'd like to see him do it again."

Willie was that type of player. He had that flair. Willie Mays! Amazing Willie!

In New York, it was Willie, Mickey, and the Duke, three excellent center fielders; Mays, Mantle, and Snider all playing in the same city at the same time. It made me wonder if Willie had not come along, would it have been Bobby, Mickey, and the Duke?

Not to brag, but I always thought I could cover as much ground in center field as anybody, including Mays. I'm not saying I should be compared with those three guys because when it came to hitting, I know I wasn't in their class. My hitting wasn't consistent enough.

It's redundant to recite Mays's numbers—the .302 lifetime batting average, the 660 home runs, the 1,903 RBIs, the 338 stolen bases. You can't reduce a career like he had to statistics. He was one of a kind.

Was he the greatest player of all time? I can't say because I never saw Babe Ruth or Ty Cobb.

The best I ever saw?

I played with Henry Aaron and I saw Joe DiMaggio, so that's a tough choice to make. Aaron had those wonderful loose hands and when I went to Milwaukee and I played with him, I'd see him hit line drives off the wall. I remember thinking to myself, "He's hitting line drives off the wall, but if he could get that ball up, they're home runs." And, of course, later he started getting the ball in the air and he did hit home runs, 755 of them.

Hank had a good arm and he could run when he wanted to. When he had a chance to beat out a hit he ran twice as fast, and we used to kid him about that. Willie had one way to play, all out all the time. Hank wasn't as flashy.

I've always been a Joe DiMaggio fan. I was such an admirer of DiMaggio, how he made it look so easy, hitting in Yankee Stadium. I admired Willie and Aaron, but DiMaggio was in a class by himself in so many ways. His grace. His elegance.

Who was the greatest? Maybe you think it's DiMaggio. Maybe you think it's Aaron. Maybe you think it's Mays. In my view, you can't go wrong with any of the three, so whichever one you choose, you'll get no argument from me.

His real name is Charles Theodore Davis, but when he was a boy in his native Kingston, Jamaica, he got a haircut that was so bad, people said it looked like he was wearing a chili bowl on his head. Before long, his friends began calling him Chili and that's how he became **Chili Davis.**

Chili was a fine-looking player, tall, rangy, and powerfully built, a switch-hitter with power who holds a record for hitting home runs from each side of the plate in the same game 11 times. He could run, he could hit, he had a great arm, and he had a very productive 19-year major league career, with 350 home runs, 142 stolen bases, and more than 1,300 RBIs. His only problem was that he couldn't catch a fly ball, which is not a very good thing if you're a center fielder.

Davis led National League outfielders in assists in 1982 and in errors four years later, which explains why after seven years in San Francisco he played the remainder of his career in the American League. Used mostly as a designated hitter, he had his best years in the AL, a high of 112 RBIs with the Angels in 1993, a high batting average of .318 with the Angels in 1995, and a high in home runs with 30 for Kansas City in 1997.

But those first seven years with the Giants were pretty good ones, too, a combined batting average of .269, an average of a shade under 70 RBIs, 17 homers, and 16 stolen bases a year. And for that, I put him number two on my list of all-time Giants center fielders.

Admittedly, that's a huge drop-off from number one, but surprisingly for a franchise that had so many great players and more Hall of Famers than any

Chili Davis (left, with Joe Morgan) averaged .267 and 17 home runs in his six full seasons with the Giants. *Photo courtesy of Bettmann/CORBIS.*

other team, the Giants, through the years, had a noticeable lack of consistent center fielders for any stretch of time until Willie Mays came along in 1951.

On the surface, the list of those who played center field for the Giants is an impressive one. It includes Roger Bresnahan, Casey Stengel, Hack Wilson, Billy Southworth, Edd Roush, Mel Ott, Freddie Lindstrom, Frank Demaree, Wiillard Marshall, Whitey Lockman, and even some kid from Glasgow, Scotland. But some made their reputation with other teams, or at another position, and none played center field for the Giants for more than two seasons.

Hank Leiber gets my vote as number three all-time Giants center fielder mostly for his relative longevity at the position, five seasons, two of which were pennant-winning years. I never saw Leiber play, but I heard about him when I joined the Giants. He was a big, strong power hitter who had some pretty good years, but not a very long career.

He had played in only 69 games for the Giants when Bill Terry made him his center fielder in 1935, and Leiber had such a tremendous year, the Giants were convinced they had a future star who would be there for many years. He batted .331, hit 22 home runs, and was fifth in the National League in RBIs with 107. Unfortunately, in the next three years with the Giants, Leiber never again came close to any of those numbers, largely because of injuries. Over those three years, he would play in only 250 games, never bat higher than .293, never hit more than 12 home runs, and never drive in more than 67 runs, although he was part of a team that won back-to-back pennants, in 1936 and 1937, and was involved in one of the most storied plays in World Series history.

It came in the Polo Grounds in the ninth inning of the second game of the '36 Series against the Yankees. The Giants had won Game 1 behind Carl Hubbell, but the Yankees put a serious hurting on the Giants in Game 2 and were leading, 18–4. With two outs, Leiber hit a towering drive to deepest center field, some 450 feet away. With his typical style and grace, Joe DiMaggio tracked the drive, raced after it, and caught up with it just in front of the center-field fence. Joe simply reached up nonchalantly, caught the ball, and ran right up the short flight of steps that led to the clubhouses.

The Giants traded Leiber to the Cubs after the 1938 season, and he had a slight resurgence in Chicago, batting .310 in 1939 with 24 homers and 88 RBIs, and .302 in 1940 with 17 homers and 86 RBIs. But he continued to be plagued by injuries and would get in only 111 games over the next two years (58 of them for the Giants in 1942) and then call it a career.

Hank Leiber is shown escorting two fans on a jeep ride to the Army Relief Fund Baseball Game at the Polo Grounds on July 30, 1942.

Benny Kauff, a name from the deep, dark, distant past, had the ability to be a big star in the major leagues if his career hadn't hit a couple of bumps, at its beginning and end.

Kauff broke into the major leagues for five games in 1912 with the Yankees (they were the Highlanders then). He came to bat 11 times and had three hits but was sent back to the minor leagues. Meanwhile, as baseball was catching on, a group of businessmen decided to form a third major league, called the Federal League. These entrepreneurs made no pretense about competing with the major leagues at first and even respected major league contracts. But they welcomed any player who was looking for an opportunity to play and grow with the new league.

Benny Kauff was one such player. Frustrated with his inability to crack the Highlanders lineup, Kauff signed on with the Indianapolis Hoosiers and

Benny Kauff had a couple of productive seasons for the Giants, batting .308 and helping them to the World Series in 1917, but he was banned from the game at the age of 30. *Photo courtesy of the Rucker Archive.*

became their best player, leading the fledging league in batting (.370), hits (211), doubles (44), runs (120), and stolen bases (75) and helping the Hoosiers win the first Federal League championship.

When the Hoosiers requested permission to move their franchise to Newark, the league granted their wish, but only with the proviso that the Hoosiers transfer Kauff's contract to the Brooklyn Tip Tops (so named because the team's owner also owned Tip Top bread).

In Brooklyn, Kauff continued to tear up the league, winning his second straight batting title with a .342 average, again leading the league in stolen bases with 55 and being hailed as "the Ty Cobb of the Federal League."

Realizing they could not compete with the American and National leagues, owners disbanded the Federal League after only two seasons and sold off their best players to the established major leagues. John McGraw of the Giants picked the prize plum by paying Brooklyn $35,000 for the contract of Kauff, who had once boasted, "I'll make Ty Cobb look like a bush leaguer if I can play for the Giants."

Although he was no Ty Cobb, Kauff had five productive years with the Giants. In 1917, he batted .308 and stole 30 bases and hit two home runs in the fourth game of the World Series against the White Sox. In New York, Kauff took up with a disreputable crowd and in 1920 he was implicated in a stolen car ring. Kauff was cleared of criminal charges, but as he did in the case of the 1919 "Black Sox" scandal, Commissioner Kenesaw Mountain Landis disregarded the judgment of the court and banned Kauff from baseball for life, cutting his career short in its prime at age 30.

What separated Willie Mays from the pack was his all-around game. He was, as baseball people like to say, a five-tool player—he could hit for average, hit for power, run, throw, and field with the best who ever played the game. When it came to just playing center field, many have been put in Mays's class, and at the head of that class was **Garry Maddox,** who was called "the Secretary of Defense."

Maddox broke into the major leagues with the Giants in 1972. The next year, he batted a lusty .319 with 11 home runs and 76 RBIs. But when he slipped to .284-8-50 in 1974, the Giants, looking for more power, dealt him to the Phillies for left-handed slugger Willie Montanez.

Perhaps the Giants acted too hastily. Maddox spent 12 seasons with the Phillies, won eight consecutive Gold Gloves, more than any other outfielder

Garry Maddox
succeeded Willie Mays
as the league's premier
center fielder, and he
was in Mays's class
defensively. *Photo
courtesy of the National
Baseball Hall of Fame.*

108

except Roberto Clemente and, of course, Mays, and became the premier center fielder in the game.

What I especially liked about Maddox was his range and his willingness to play shallow, which allowed him to cut off hits on balls hit in front of him. It's one of my pet peeves that too many outfielders like to play deep to avoid the embarrassment of balls hit over their head and as a result they'd be unable to do anything but watch as balls fell in front of them. By playing shallow, that was never a problem for Maddox. With his speed and long-legged gait, neither was having balls hit over his head.

As Hall of Famer Ralph Kiner, the longtime broadcaster for the Mets, once said, "Two-thirds of the earth is covered by water, the other one-third is covered by Garry Maddox."

Statistical Summaries

All statistics are for player's Giants career only.

HITTING

G = Games

H = Hits

HR = Home runs

RBI = Runs batted in

SB = Stolen bases

BA = Batting average

Center Fielder	Years	G	H	HR	RBI	SB	BA
Willie Mays *Missed only 26 of Giants' 1,536 games between 1954 and 1963*	1951–52, 1954–72	2,857	3,187	646	1,859	336	.304
Chili Davis *Drew 23 intentional walks in 1986, second most in the NL*	1981–87	874	840	101	418	95	.267
Hank Leiber *Pitched a complete game (9–1 loss to Philadelphia) in only mound appearance on September 25, 1942*	1933–38, 1942	531	527	53	319	3	.287

continued	Years	G	H	HR	RBI	SB	BA
Benny Kauff *Had an unassisted double play against Chicago on July 19, 1916*	1916–20	564	582	29	274	103	.287
Garry Maddox *Had third-highest batting average in NL (.319) in his 1973 rookie season*	1972–75	421	469	32	188	59	.287

FIELDING

PO = Putouts

A = Assists

E = Errors

DP = Double plays

TC/G = Total chances divided by games played

FA = Fielding average

Center Fielder	PO	A	E	DP	TC/G	FA
Willie Mays	6,883	190	137	59	2.6	.981
Chili Davis	1,907	57	52	13	2.9	.974
Hank Leiber	976	27	30	10	2.2	.971
Benny Kauff	1,250	73	53	17	2.5	.961
Garry Maddox	1,031	17	23	3	2.6	.979

EIGHT

Right Fielder

You can probably imagine how excited I was to be called up to the major leagues in 1946. Like any young kid the first time he steps onto a big league field, Wow! He's walking in heaven. Here I was a kid of 23, not only playing big league baseball, but playing in the city where I grew up for the team I rooted for as a boy. As if that wasn't enough to excite me, I was going to be a teammate of my boyhood hero, **Mel Ott,** and he was also my manager. I was nervous just talking to him.

1. MEL OTT

2. BOBBY BONDS

3. ROSS YOUNGS

4. DON MUELLER

5. FELIPE ALOU

A kid breaking into the big leagues couldn't play for a better manager than Ott. He was kind, gentle, soft-spoken, easygoing, understanding, and considerate. He was somebody I admired, just a nice, nice man, a decent man, a well-respected man. Mel was a gentleman, honorable, sincere, and warm-hearted. Any nice things you can say about a guy, you can say about Mel Ott. That's the way I felt about him. He treated me like the young, innocent guy I was, and I have never forgotten it.

It was Ott whom Leo Durocher was talking about when he said, "Nice guys finish last."

Mel Ott spent his entire 22-year Hall of Fame career with the Giants, making his debut in 1926 at the age of 17.

And Ott did finish last as a manager twice, in 1943 and 1946. Except for his first year—1942, when he replaced Bill Terry and finished in third place—Ott never finished higher than fourth in his seven seasons as manager of the Giants.

One day we were playing in Cincinnati and we were killing them. We were getting hit after hit and Ott was on the bench. We got another hit and another hit, and Ott just sat back and laughed like he was a little kid enjoying the game. I didn't think anything of it at the time, but later when I thought back to that day, it made me realize what a nice guy he was. He wasn't as cutthroat as, say, Leo Durocher, which is why Ott wasn't a very good manager. A good guy, but you're not going to win with him like you would with Durocher.

When I got to the Giants, Ott was winding down a fabulous career. He was still an active player, but he didn't play too much. Mostly, he used himself as a pinch-hitter. I don't remember him playing right field while I was there. He might have played a game or two, but I can't remember.

Of course, Ott had that unorthodox hitting style where he would pick up his front leg. It was unusual, but we just accepted it. You would think a change-up would screw up his mechanics, but it didn't. He had the ability to wait long enough, time it right, stay back, and knock it. And he hit in the perfect park. He'd get on top of the ball and hook it into the right-field seats, just 257 feet away.

He wasn't a big guy, just 5'9", 170 pounds, but he hit a lot of home runs—511 of them. Sure there were a lot of Polo Grounders in there, but he didn't hit all 511 homers in the Polo Grounds. It's surprising that with all the success he had, nobody ever tried to hit like that. He was the only one, but look at how many hitters do it today.

Ott came out of the small town of Gretna, Louisiana, a suburb of New Orleans, to become one of the biggest stars and most beloved figures in the history of New York baseball. He was playing semi-pro ball at the age of 16 when a local businessman who owned several semi-pro teams in the area saw him play. The owner recommended Ott to John McGraw, who invited the youngster to New York for a tryout with the Giants, watched him rocket long drives into the Polo Grounds' upper-right-field deck and hammer line drives into the gaps, and signed him on the spot.

Other players and sportswriters looked at Ott's unorthodox hitting style and mocked Ott. Even McGraw talked to Mel about changing his style.

"Why do you raise your right leg as you start your swing?" McGraw inquired.

"I always hit that way, Mr. McGraw," Ott replied. "I guess it just comes natural to me."

"Then keep right on hitting that way," the manager said. "Don't let anybody change you."

Ott was a catcher at the time, but McGraw, recognizing Mel's hitting promise, wisely had him abandon catching rather than risk him wearing down physically at such a strenuous position. McGraw had Ott work out at third base, second base, and center field before settling on him as a right fielder.

McGraw ignored suggestions that he send the youngster to the minor leagues for seasoning. "Ott stays with me," he said, and planted Ott on the bench alongside him so McGraw could impart his wisdom and his experience on the young man. Consequently, Ott never played a game in the minor leagues.

He made his debut in 1926 at the age of 17 years, one month, and 25 days. Used mostly as a pinch-hitter, Mel appeared in 35 games, batted 60 times, and had 23 hits, a .383 average. Two years later, at the age of 19, he was the Giants regular right fielder. Sportswriters dubbed him "Master Melvin" as Ott batted .322, hit 18 home runs, and drove in 77 in his first full season. By 1929, he was a full-fledged star at the age of 20, batting .328, hitting 42 home runs (one behind the National League leader, Chuck Klein), driving in 151 runs (eight behind the league leader, Hack Wilson), while leading the league with 113 walks.

Ott would lead the league in home runs six times, in RBIs once, and in bases on balls six times in his 22-year career, all of them with the Giants. When he retired in 1947, he had a lifetime batting average of .304, more than 1,800 RBIs and runs scored, more than 1,700 walks, and those 511 home runs that stood as the National League record for 20 years until it was broken by another Giant, Willie Mays.

When Bill Terry stepped down as manager of the Giants after the 1941 season, Terry and owner Horace Stoneham agreed that Ott was the logical successor. But Mel was miscast, and unprepared, to be a manager. His biggest problem was his laid-back style and nice-guy image. When he attempted to step out of character and get tough, it was obviously forced and disingenuous, and that contributed to his downfall.

After he was replaced by, of all people, Leo Durocher, in 1948, Ott stayed on and worked with his close friend and former roommate, Carl Hubbell, running the Giants' farm system. When his contract ran out in 1950, Ott managed the Oakland Oaks of the Pacific Coast League for two seasons, and then became a radio broadcaster with the Detroit Tigers.

In November of 1958, returning home from dinner with his wife, Ott's car was struck head-on by a drunken driver. He sustained multiple injuries and died a few days later. He was only 49.

Bobby Bonds, Barry's dad, had the promise and the talent—a rare combination of power and speed—to be one of baseball's greatest players ever, a certain Hall of Famer. Although he had an outstanding 14-year major league career, with 332 home runs, 461 stolen bases, and more than 1,000 RBIs— Bobby never quite lived up to his potential. Baseball people always said he should have done much better.

One problem was that Bonds played almost all of his San Francisco years in the shadow of Willie Mays, the player Bonds idolized. The two became good friends (Bonds even asked Willie to be godfather to his son, Barry), but comparisons were inevitable and people expected Bonds to be another Willie Mays, especially after he broke in with the Giants on June 25, 1968, by hitting a grand-slam home run in the sixth inning against the Dodgers in Candlestick Park, making him the only player in the 20th century to hit a grand slam for his first major league hit.

But Bobby was not another Willie. He could not be another Willie. There was only one Willie Mays.

Bonds's other fatal flaw was his penchant for strikeouts. He collected them by the carload, 187 in 1969, a major league record, which he increased to 189 the following year. For his career, Bonds had almost as many strikeouts (1,757) as he had base hits (1,886).

Rather than dwell on what Bonds didn't do, I prefer to concentrate on what he did, like becoming the first player in baseball history with three 30/30 seasons, 30 home runs and 30 stolen bases; combining with son Barry to hold the record for the most home runs by a father-son duo; being one of only two players in baseball history (the other is his son, Barry) with 400 stolen bases and 300 home runs; and setting a major league record, since broken by Rickey Henderson, by hitting 35 home runs leading off a game.

Many people thought it was a waste to have a hitter with such power as a leadoff batter and a few managers tried hitting Bobby in the number three hole, but he never seemed comfortable batting third and he always produced better numbers hitting leadoff.

After spending his first seven seasons with the Giants, Bonds played the last seven seasons of his career with seven different teams. Those teams were seduced by Bobby's enormous natural ability, but they soon tired of his strikeouts.

Bobby Bonds was a special kind of player, but he probably suffered a little bit by playing in the shadow of his very dear friend Willie Mays.

Giants baseball has long been a family affair, from Charles A. Stoneham, who purchased the team in 1919 and ran the team until his death in 1936, to Stoneham's son, Horace, who was elected president of the Giants upon his father's death and, at 33, became the youngest man ever to head a major league franchise.

In 1950 Charles A. (Chub) Feeney, Horace Stoneham's nephew and Charles Stoneham's grandson, operated the Giants as general manager until he left to become president of the National League.

Horace Stoneham served as Giants president for 40 years. In 1976, he sold the team to Bob Lurie.

Familial ties continue with the Giants to this day. Star left fielder Barry Bonds's father, Bobby, was a Giant from 1968 to 1974, and Barry's godfather is the greatest Giant of them all, Willie Mays.

Felipe Alou, the team's manager from 2003 to 2006, played for the Giants four decades earlier and played in the same outfield alongside his brothers, Matty and Jesus. And Felipe Alou's son, Moises, joined the team in 2005.

Following is a list of the most home runs in baseball history by father-son combinations, and a list of the most hits in baseball history compiled by brothers. (Editor's note: Those who wore a Giants uniform are listed in bold face. Totals are through the 2006 season.)

Most Home Runs by a Father-Son Combination
1. **Bobby Bonds** and **Barry Bonds**, 1,066
2. Ken Griffey Sr. and Ken Griffey Jr., 715
3. **Felipe Alou** and **Moises Alou**, 525
4. Bob Boone and Aaron and Bret Boone, 472
5. Tony Perez and Eduardo Perez, 458
6*t*. Gus Bell and Buddy Bell, 407
6*t*. Yogi Berra and Dale Berra, 407
8. Jose Cruz Sr. and **Jose Cruz Jr.**, 363
9. Cecil Fielder and Prince Fielder, 349
10. Sandy Alomar Sr. and Roberto Alomar and Sandy Alomar Jr., 335

11. Buddy Bell and David and Mike Bell, 326
12. **Gary Matthews Sr.** and Gary Matthews Jr., 312
13. Hal McRae and Brian McRae, 294
14. **Randy Hundley** and Todd Hundley, 284
15. Earl Averill and Earl Averill Jr., 282

Most Hits by a Combination of Brothers
1. Paul Waner and Lloyd Waner, 5,611
2. **Felipe Alou, Matty Alou,** and **Jesus Alou,** 5,094
3. Joe DiMaggio, Dom DiMaggio, and Vince DiMaggio, 4,853
4. Ed Delahanty, Frank Delahanty, **Jim Delahanty**, Joe Delahanty, and Tom Delahanty, 4,211
5. Henry Aaron and Tommie Aaron, 3,987
6. Roberto Alomar and Sandy Alomar Jr., 3,957
7. Cal Ripken Jr. and Billy Ripken, 3,858
8. Joe Sewell and Luke Sewell, 3,619
9. Ken Boyer, Clete Boyer, and Cloyd Boyer, 3,559
10. Honus Wagner and Butts Wagner, 3,474
11. Tony Gwynn and Chris Gwynn, 3,404
12. Bob Johnson and Roy Johnson, 3,343
13. Eddie Murray and **Rich Murray**, 3,299
14. George Brett and Ken Brett, 3,245
15. Bob Meusel and **Irish Meusel**, 3,214

As shocking and tragic as was Lou Gehrig's sudden demise, the same was true of **Ross Youngs,** who was at the height of a Hall of Fame career with the Giants when he was struck down by a mysterious and incurable illness a decade before Gehrig succumbed. The difference is that Youngs's malady wasn't named for him, and Hollywood didn't memorialize him in a movie.

As big a star as Gehrig was with the Yankees, Youngs was just as big a star with the Giants, with the one exception being that Youngs was not the power hitter Gehrig was; he never hit more than 10 home runs in any season, but in 10 years with the Giants he batted over .300 nine times and had a lifetime average of .322.

Only 5'8" and 162 pounds, Youngs was a slashing left-handed hitter and fearless base stealer. In 1919, he led the National League with 31 doubles. In

1920, he batted .351, second in the league to Rogers Hornsby. In 1924, his .356 average placed him third behind Hornsby and Zack Wheat. The right fielder for the Giants on four consecutive pennant-winning teams (1921–24), he had a strong and accurate throwing arm and a sprinter's speed.

On the wall behind John McGraw's desk in his office in the Polo Grounds hung two portraits, one of Christy Mathewson and the other of Youngs, who McGraw called his greatest outfielder.

Youngs was briefly touched by scandal when, after eight members of the Chicago White Sox were accused of throwing the 1919 World Series, rumors

Ross Youngs, shown scoring a run in the 1921 World Series, had a Hall of Fame career with the Giants from 1917 to 1926. Unfortunately, it was cut short by a terminal kidney ailment that took his life at the age of 30. *Photo courtesy of MLB Photos via Getty Images.*

circulated that Youngs had taken bribes from New York gamblers. His team-mate, Jimmy O'Connell, who was banned from baseball, charged Youngs with failure to report an alleged attempt to fix a game in 1924. Youngs quickly confronted the allegations and denied the charges. His reputation was so impeccable that he was acquitted of the charges and absolved of any wrongdoing.

The following season, Youngs's batting average tumbled 92 points, from .356 to .264, and suspicions were raised that the decline was the aftermath of the allegations against him. The reason for the slide became obvious the following spring when Youngs was diagnosed with Bright's disease, a terminal kidney ailment.

Despite the illness, Youngs continued to play. The Giants hired a full-time nurse to travel with him and Youngs managed to bat .306 in 95 games. But his illness progressed rapidly, leaving him debilitated and bedridden. He missed the entire 1927 season and died at his home in San Antonio on October 22, 1927, at the age of 30. He was elected to the Hall of Fame in 1972.

As a postscript, the year after Youngs's death, his right-field position was taken by a 19-year-old left-handed slugger from Louisiana named Mel Ott, leaving one to wonder how many more pennants the Giants would have won if they had both Ott and Youngs in the same outfield.

Sportswriters pinned the nickname "Mandrake" on **Don Mueller** because he was a magician with the bat. You never saw a guy get so many cheap hits, bleeders, eight hoppers through the infield, soft line drives in the gap, pop flys that fell between infielders and outfielders.

I'd be in a slump, 0–for 19, and I'd hit three balls on the nose, line drives right at fielders. Easy outs. And Mueller would dribble a few through the infield and he'd be three-for-four. It made me nuts, and it drove the opposition crazy.

Don didn't hit many home runs, only 65 in 12 seasons, only twice in double figures, and never more than 16 in any season. That wasn't his style. But he had that magic wand. He was what they call a "pure hitter." His style was to make contact, hit the ball where it was pitched, take it to the opposite field, find a gap in the outfield or a hole in the infield, and he did it with the best of them. And he rarely struck out. Only 146 strikeouts in 4,364 major league at-bats—that's one strikeout for every 29.9 at-bats. The most he ever struck out in any season was 26 times.

In 1954, Mueller batted .342 and was nosed out of the National League batting championship by Willie Mays, who hit .345. Mueller led the league with 212 hits, and in 619 at-bats he struck out only 17 times. That was a week's worth for me.

The only thing against Mueller is that he couldn't run very well and we had our little thing going on. He used to call me "the Hawk" because so many times I would range almost to right field to make catches. We still have a nice relationship, exchanging Christmas cards every year. When I played center field before Willie Mays came along, I never liked giving anybody a hit on a ball hit in front of me. So I would play a very shallow center field, but Don, because he didn't run well and was concerned about the ball going over his head, would play a deep right field. I used to get on him all the time about moving in and not letting balls fall in front of him.

Don Mueller (No. 22) tries to slide into first base but is beaten to the bag by Ted Kluszewski in a 1951 game against the Reds.

Don came by his hitting ability naturally. His father, Walter, was an out-fielder with the Pirates in the 1920s, and his uncle, Heinie, played 11 seasons in the major leagues for four teams, including the Giants. But he couldn't get along with John McGraw and was a Giant for only a short time.

Mueller is probably best remembered for the base hit he got in the ninth inning of the third playoff game against the Dodgers in 1951. Al Dark had led off the bottom of the ninth with a single and, with Gil Hodges holding Dark on base, Mueller followed with a hit past Hodges, a six-hopper, naturally. One out later, Whitey Lockman doubled and Mueller jammed his ankle sliding into third base. He had to be carried off the field on a stretcher.

As a result, Mueller missed the 1951 World Series against the Yankees, which Don said was his biggest disappointment in baseball. The two players who replaced Mueller in right field in that Series were a combined 2-for-18 without an RBI. We lost the Series, four games to two. Who knows, if Mueller had been able to play, things might have been different.

When Mueller finally got a chance to play in a World Series, in the Giants' four-game sweep of the Indians in 1954, he batted .389.

This segment on Giants right fielders might properly be called "All in the Family." It includes Bobby Bonds, father of Barry, Don Mueller, whose father and uncle were both major league outfielders, and **Felipe Alou,** whose two brothers were major league outfielders and whose son, Moises, is also a major league outfielder.

In a few games in 1963, the Giants outfield consisted of all three Alou brothers, Felipe, Matty, and Jesus, the only time in baseball history that has happened. In fact, at one point in a game against the Mets, they batted in succession in the same inning.

Felipe was the oldest, and the only power hitter of the three Alou brothers, with 206 homers (brothers Matty and Jesus had only 63 homers between them in more than 10,000 at-bats). But Matty, a lefty-batting slap-and-run hitter, had a lifetime batting average of .307 (21 points higher than Felipe) and won a National League batting championship in 1966 with the Pirates.

With the Giants, Felipe batted over .300 just once with a .316 average in 1962. He later batted .327 and .317 with Atlanta.

Felipe is the only one of the Alou brothers to stay in baseball after his playing days. He had been outspoken against the presumed boycott of minorities

Felipe Alou, shown here leaping in vain for a Hank Aaron home run, is the oldest member of one of baseball's most famous families.

in the role of manager. Felipe finally got his chance with Montreal in 1992 and spent 10 successful years as manager of the Expos, finishing first once and second three times and being named National League Manager of the Year in 1994.

After sitting out a season, in 2003 Felipe was named manager of the Giants, a position he held for four seasons.

Statistical Summaries

All statistics are for player's Giants career only.

HITTING

G = Games
H = Hits
HR = Home runs
RBI = Runs batted in
SB = Stolen bases
BA = Batting average

Right Fielder	Years	G	H	HR	RBI	SB	BA
Mel Ott *Twice scored a record six runs in one game (August 4, 1934, April 30, 1944)*	1926–47	2,730	2,876	511	1,860	89	.304
Bobby Bonds *MVP of 1973 All-Star Game*	1968–74	1,014	1,106	186	552	263	.273
Ross Youngs *Had three triples in one game on May 11, 1920*	1917–26	1,211	1,491	42	592	153	.322

continued	Years	G	H	HR	RBI	SB	BA
Don Mueller *Had seven hits and scored four runs in Giants' 1954 World Series sweep over Cleveland*	1948–57	1,171	1,248	65	504	11	.298
Felipe Alou *Had nine consecutive hits during 1962 season*	1958–63	719	655	85	325	51	.286

FIELDING

PO = Putouts

A = Assists

E = Errors

DP = Double plays

TC/G = Total chances divided by games played

FA = Fielding average

Right Fielder	PO	A	E	DP	TC/G	FA
Mel Ott	4,511	256	98	60	2.1	.980
Bobby Bonds	2,159	70	55	22	2.3	.976
Ross Youngs	2,160	191	116	47	2.1	.953
Don Mueller	1,759	66	33	19	1.8	.982
Felipe Alou	1,130	35	26	7	1.8	.978

NINE

Right-Handed Pitcher

When it comes to choosing the greatest right-handed pitcher in Giants history, this is a no-brainer.

I didn't have to see **Christy Mathewson** pitch to realize he deserves to be number one. Just look at his record:

- 373 wins, tied with Grover Cleveland Alexander for third all-time behind Cy Young and Walter Johnson
- A career earned-run average of 2.13, fifth best all-time
- 435 complete games in 552 starts
- Four seasons of 30 wins or more (a high of 37 in 1908, third most all-time), and 12 consecutive seasons with 20 wins or more
- 80 shutouts, third all-time
- 2,502 strikeouts
- 846 walks in 4,782 innings, or .63 walks every nine innings
- Three shutouts and 14 hits allowed in the 1905 World Series

1. CHRISTY MATHEWSON
2. JUAN MARICHAL
3. GAYLORD PERRY
4. SAL MAGLIE
5. LARRY JANSEN

Christy Mathewson, shown circa 1910, is regarded as one of the greatest pitchers of all time and was a charter member of the Hall of Fame when it opened in 1936.

I know the game has changed and Mathewson played in an era—just after the turn of the 20ᵗʰ century—where pitching dominated and the rules favored pitchers, but how are you going to ignore numbers like that?

The great Connie Mack, who saw them all in his more than 50 years in the game, once said Mathewson "was the greatest pitcher who ever lived. He had knowledge, judgment, perfect control, and form. It was wonderful to watch him pitch when he wasn't pitching against you."

Another thing I learned about Matty—his nickname was "Big Six" after New York's most famous fire engine—is the tremendous contribution he made toward bringing credibility and acceptance to professional baseball players at a time when they were considered lowlife, shiftless, lazy, ne'er-do-wells.

Back then, ballplayers were known for being carousers and hard-drinking tobacco-chewers. Most of them came from the country or the poorer sections of big cities. They lacked education and sophistication, were thought to have no ambition and no trade, so they turned to baseball. The old line was, "You wouldn't want your daughter to marry a baseball player."

Mathewson changed all that. He was college educated and polished, and at 6'2" tall, 195 pounds, blonde hair and blue eyes and handsome, he was the all-American boy, the perfect role model for youngsters and he became the idol of thousands.

Mathewson, the son of a Pennsylvania farmer, had attended Bucknell University, where he sang in the glee club, was class president, kicked field goals for the football team, and was the star pitcher on the baseball team. He was at the forefront of an attempt by baseball players to form a union in 1912, and later enlisted in the army as a captain during World War I.

Historians also have credited Mathewson with being responsible, at least indirectly, for one of baseball's great nicknames. It came in the 1911 World Series between the Giants and Philadelphia Athletics.

Athletics third baseman Frank Baker, who led the American League in home runs with 11 and was considered the premier power hitter of his day, had hit a two-run home run off Rube Marquard in the sixth inning of Game 2 to give Philadelphia a 3–1 victory. The following day, Baker struck again. He hit a home run off Mathewson in the ninth inning to tie the score and send the game into extra innings.

Two home runs in the same World Series was rare and fans, in awe of the Athletics third baseman's power display, began to refer to him as "Home Run" Baker, a name that stayed with him for the rest of his life, and beyond.

Because of John McGraw's bombastic, rambunctious personality and his hell-for-leather, tyrannical, pugnacious style as a manager, it would seem that he and Mathewson would be incompatible, but just the opposite was the case. Maybe because opposites attract, McGraw and Mathewson became the closest of friends, a baseball odd couple. McGraw often referred to Matty as "my adopted son."

In 1899, Mathewson left Bucknell to try his hand as a pitcher. After two minor league seasons, the Giants purchased his contract from Norfolk for $1,500, but when he lost his first three decisions in 1900, the Giants cancelled the deal and demanded their money back. Mathewson was drafted by Cincinnati for $100, and after the 1900 season, the Giants traded Amos Rusie to reacquire Mathewson in what many old-time observers say was the greatest (or worst, from Cincinnati's perspective) trade in baseball history.

Rusie had had a Hall of Fame career with the Giants just before the 20th century, winning 233 games in eight seasons and losing only 163. But he was 39 years old when the Reds got him, and he had not pitched in two years. He wouldn't win a game for the Reds, while Mathewson became a huge star.

Back with the Giants, Mathewson won 20 games and pitched a no-hitter in 1901, but for some reason, the following year Horace Fogel took over as manager of the Giants and figured that Matty, a good hitter, would best serve the Giants as a position player. Fogel tried Mathewson in the outfield and at first base without success, and Matty's pitching suffered as he won only 14 games and lost 17.

By July, Fogel was gone, John McGraw had taken over as manager, and Mathewson's career as a position player had ended. Matty responded by winning 30 games in 1903, his first of 12 consecutive seasons with 20 or more wins.

That run of success ended in 1915, when Mathewson won only eight games and lost 14. Midway through the following season, struggling with a record of 3–4, Mathewson was traded to the Reds. It was not so much banishment as it was a gesture by McGraw, who positioned his friend to take over as Cincinnati's manager.

Mathewson's stint as a manager was none too successful. In two and a half seasons, he lost more games than he won and never finished higher than fourth.

But Mathewson's failure as a manager could not detract from his enormous success as a pitcher and one of the great players of all time.

In 1936, when the Baseball Hall of Fame opened in Cooperstown, New York, five players were inducted as charter members. Christy Mathewson was one of the five. The other four were Babe Ruth, Ty Cobb, Honus Wagner, and Walter Johnson.

Juan Marichal's first year in the major leagues was my last, and since I was in the American League at the time, with Boston and Baltimore, I never got to hit against him. For that I'm thankful.

Marichal had to be tough to hit against, as his record attests, 243 wins and 142 losses in 16 years, a career earned-run average of 2.89, six 20-win seasons. He threw four outstanding pitches: curveball, slider, screwball, and an overpowering fastball. And he threw them at different speeds, with different deliveries and several release points, making it seem like he went to the mound armed with 15 or 16 pitches.

He also had pinpoint control (only 709 walks and 2,303 strikeouts in more than 3,500 innings). To top it all off, he had this high kick that allowed him to hide the ball, added to his deception, and made him especially tough against right-handed batters.

Juan Marichal's high leg-kick and his ability to hide the ball during his delivery made him especially tough on hitters, resulting in 243 wins over 16 seasons.

As if that wasn't enough, he was a workhorse who pitched more than 300 innings in a season three times. In 1963, when he led the National League in wins with 25 and innings pitched with 321⅓, he dueled Warren Spahn in a classic battle. Both pitched complete games and Marichal and the Giants won, 1–0, on a home run by Willie Mays in the sixteenth inning.

Spahn was 42 at the time, Marichal 25, and the story goes that Giants manager Alvin Dark kept trying to take Marichal out of the game, but Juan kept refusing to leave.

"I just didn't want to leave before he did," Marichal said. "I didn't want that old man lasting longer than me."

Marichal became an immediate favorite of San Francisco fans. In his first major league game, he pitched a one-hit shutout against the Phillies, the only hit coming on a pinch-hit single in the eighth. Four days later, he pitched a four-hitter against the Pirates.

From 1962 through 1969, pitching in a league that also had Sandy Koufax and Bob Gibson, Marichal won 172 games, led the league in wins twice, winning percentage once, complete games twice, ERA once, innings pitched twice, and shutouts twice.

Unfortunately, the one thing many people remember about Marichal is an incident that happened in 1965, in a game against the Dodgers. Two days before, the two teams almost had a brawl on the field (yes, the hostilities between them that started in New York and Brooklyn carried over to San Francisco and Los Angeles).

Pitching against Koufax, Marichal had knocked down Maury Wills and Ron Fairly. Dodgers catcher John Roseboro wanted Koufax to retaliate by hitting Marichal when Juan came to bat. Koufax reportedly refused, so Roseboro took matters into his own hands. In returning the ball to the mound, Roseboro threw it close to Marichal's ear (deliberately, many believe). There were words and the next thing you knew, Roseboro took off his mask and stood up to confront Marichal, who brought his bat down right on Roseboro's head.

That's when all hell broke loose. Players from both teams poured onto the field, fists were thrown, and there were skirmishes all over the place.

Marichal was fined $1,750 and suspended for a week. He missed two starts and the Giants finished two games behind the Dodgers.

Roseboro, who suffered a concussion, sued Marichal, but later he dropped the suit.

There was a happy ending to this ugly incident. Years later, Marichal and Roseboro buried the hatchet and became friends. When Marichal failed to be elected to the Hall of Fame in his first two years of eligibility, Roseboro campaigned for Juan's election. Marichal made it in his third year and in his acceptance speech he made sure to thank Roseboro for his support.

What are we to make of **Gaylord Perry**? Was he a cheater who won 314 major league games and was elected to the Hall of Fame by using an illegal pitch? Or was he a great pitcher and an equally adept actor who made people think he was cheating just to get an edge on hitters?

The fact that his autobiography was titled *Me and the Spitter*, might be considered an indictment, but Perry never admitted in the book that he actually threw the illegal pitch. Whether he did or didn't, he encouraged others to

Gaylord Perry was outstanding during the first 10 years of his career as a Giant, but it was after we traded him away that he won Cy Young Awards, with Cleveland and San Diego.

believe he was loading up the baseball by fidgeting on the mound, touching different parts of his uniform, his cap, his face, his glove, his socks before delivering a pitch.

That put the idea of a spitter in the hitter's mind, and it worked for Gaylord. Opposing hitters and rival managers were always complaining and asking the umpires to inspect the pitcher. Umpires would go to the mound and practically undress Gaylord, looking for grease, jelly, or Vaseline. But they never found anything.

Meanwhile, Perry continued to win. He led his league in wins for three different teams—in 1970 with the Giants (for whom he pitched the first 10 years of his major league career and won 134 games), in 1972 with the Indians, and in 1978 with the Padres. He won 20 or more games in a season five times, pitched 300 or more innings six times, struck out 3,534 batters, and is the only pitcher to win Cy Young Awards in each league, with Cleveland in 1972 and San Diego in 1978.

When Perry slipped from 23 wins in 1970 to 16 in 1971, the Giants figured his best days were behind him and traded him to Cleveland for Sam McDowell, who would win only 11 games in a Giants uniform. Meanwhile, Perry would pitch 12 more seasons and win 180 more games for seven different teams.

They called **Sal Maglie** "the Barber," not so much because of his dark complexion and quickly growing beard that gave him a perpetual five o'clock shadow, although that was part of how he got his nickname. Mainly it was for his penchant for throwing close to batters, to give them a close shave with the baseball.

"When I'm pitching," Sal used to say, "I own the plate."

You might think to look at him that Sal was a mean man, and he was, but only when he was on the mound. Otherwise, he was gentle and soft-spoken. I never thought of Barber as a mean guy. He used to laugh at his reputation for meanness.

But put a baseball in his hand and he could be vicious, especially against the Dodgers, our archenemies. He was known as a Dodger killer. They used to say that all Maglie had to do was throw his glove on the mound and the Dodgers would be beat. Carl Furillo, the Dodgers' right fielder, used to complain a lot about Maglie throwing at him and their battles were the stuff of legend, but I always thought it was more a Furillo-Durocher thing than a

Sal Maglie was best known for his nasty, hard-nosed demeanor on the pitcher's mound, but off the field he was a gentle, soft-spoken man.

Furillo-Maglie thing. The proof of that is when Maglie joined the Dodgers, he and Furillo became teammates and I hear they got along well.

Back then, there was a lot of throwing at hitters. If one of our players got hit by a pitch, Leo Durocher used to say, "Don't show them that it bothers you; don't rub it." Durocher's credo was "don't get mad, get even."

One time we were scheduled to face the Dodgers in a big three-game series, Friday, Saturday, Sunday, at the Polo Grounds, and Maglie was set to pitch the opener. One local paper trumpeted the game with a headline that said something like "Maglie to Deck Dodgers."

Durocher didn't have many meetings, but this time, because of the headlines, he called a meeting before the first game and he said, "Forget all that stuff. Just go out there and play our game." And then he said, "But"—there was always a "but" with Leo—"as soon as one of their guys comes up inside, I want two-for-one." Leo was a two-for-one guy. In other words, if one of our guys went down, he wanted his pitcher to knock down two of their guys.

Maglie had this reputation for pitching high and tight and he used that to his advantage. He knew he intimidated hitters and that became a big weapon for him. The fact is, sometimes when hitters thought he was throwing at them intentionally, it was really because he'd thrown a curveball that didn't break. He could throw some bad curveballs. Playing behind him in center field, I saw Sal get by with a lot of spinners, curveballs that didn't break. When he threw the good ones—and he threw a lot of good ones—he was tough and his reputation helped him a lot.

One reason Sal was so successful against the Dodgers is that they had a lineup loaded with right-handed hitters and Maglie had that hellacious curveball. He'd come in tight with his fastball on those strong right-handed hitters to knock them off the plate and they'd be thinking fastball high and inside and Sal would throw that great curveball and the Dodgers would wave futilely at it.

Maglie learned the curveball from an old Cuban pitcher named Adolfo Luque, who he met when Sal was playing in the outlaw Mexican League.

That was in 1946, and was one of the sad chapters in baseball's history. At the time there were no agents, no free agency, no arbitration, and major league players were grossly underpaid. The minimum salary for a major leaguer was $4,000.

A wealthy Mexican named Jorge Pasquel decided he was going to challenge the major league's monopoly and form a league that would rival the majors. To do so, he raided major league teams of players, offering them contracts that doubled and tripled their American salaries. Pasquel enticed 23 players to jump to the Mexican League. Maglie was one of the 23.

As a result, all 23 players were branded outlaws by major league baseball and were banned from ever playing again in American organized baseball. That ban was later rescinded and those players were allowed to return to organized baseball in the United States.

At the time, Maglie had been a mediocre pitcher for the Giants, with a 5–4 record in his only season, 1945.

In Mexico, Maglie came under the tutelage of Luque and perfected his curveball. When he was finally allowed to return to the Giants in 1950, Sal was a different pitcher. He was a mature 33 years old by then, and with the experience he gained in Mexico and the lessons he learned from Luque, his transformation was miraculous.

In his first year back, Maglie was 18–4 and led the National League with a winning percentage of .818. The following year, he and Larry Jansen tied for the league lead in wins with 23, and in 1952, Sal was 18–8.

Maglie was a big part of New York baseball and of the great Giants-Dodgers rivalry in the 1950s.

After I was traded to the Braves, I remember going into the Polo Grounds to play the Giants and Maglie was pitching. He threw me a fastball on the fists and I swung and hit a high lazy fly ball to left field that just got into the seats; a typical Polo Grounds home run, right down the line.

I was happy to get it. But I was kind of embarrassed. I ran around the bases and I never looked up until I got to the dugout, sat down, and then I looked up, and there was Maglie, still standing on the mound waiting for me to look at him and for our eyes to meet. And he said, "Hey, next time…" and he made a gesture with his hand across his chin as if to say he intended to knock me down.

That was Sal the Barber.

For the first five years of his career, **Larry Jansen,** another of my roommates, was as good a pitcher as there was in the major leagues. In those five years, he won 96 games and lost only 57.

Larry was almost 27 when he came to the Giants, and he broke in spectacularly, a record of 21–5, a league-leading winning percentage of .808, and 20 complete games. He had a good fastball, a great curveball, and excellent control. At one point, he had 10 straight complete-game victories, and after one of them, catcher Walker Cooper was quoted as saying, "I don't believe he missed the target by more than two inches all day."

Larry might have been Rookie of the Year in the National League, but that was the year Jackie Robinson broke in with such a flourish and with all that publicity. Jansen finished second to Robinson in the voting.

In 1951, Jansen combined with Sal Maglie to give the Giants a strong one-two pitching combination and he and Sal were largely responsible for our comeback that allowed us to catch the Dodgers.

When you have two pitchers like that, you can avoid long losing streaks, and that's what Maglie and Jansen did for us, especially in the second half of the season.

*I*n the Giants' pennant-winning season of 1951, Larry Jansen and Sal Maglie combined to win 46 games and form the most potent one-two pitching tandem in baseball. They were teammates and friends and good-natured rivals, competing against one another for the league lead in victories, and to make things interesting they agreed on a friendly little wager on who would win the most games, all to the benefit of the Giants.

"I was chasing Sal all season," Jansen remembered. "I kept telling him, 'I'm going to catch you,' and he kept saying, 'No you won't.'"

When Jansen beat Boston on the final day of the regular season, it was his 22nd victory. Maglie had 23. But the bet, and the pennant, still was not decided. The Dodgers and Giants were tied, necessitating a three-game playoff. There still was a chance for Jansen, but only a slim one.

Having pitched the final regular season game on a Sunday, he would not get a start in the playoff. Maglie was penciled in to start Game 3...if there was a Game 3. Jansen needed a miracle. What he got was a home run by Bobby Thomson.

With the playoff tied, one game each, Maglie started the third game in the Polo Grounds. He pitched well, but without much luck. When the Dodgers scored three runs in the top of the eighth to take a 4–1 lead, it looked like the pennant and Jansen's bet would both go down the drain.

But the Giants refused to quit, and neither did their manager, Leo Durocher. He brought in Jansen, his co-pitching ace, to pitch the ninth inning despite a three-run deficit. It seemed at the time a futile gesture.

"I remember the Dodgers yelling at me from their dugout—'Pack your bags, Jansen...Where are you going to be pitching tomorrow?'" said Jansen, who retired the Dodgers in order in the top of the ninth, and waited for his miracle. It came with one swing of Bobby Thomson's bat.

Jansen recalled:

> *When I got into the clubhouse, the first guy I saw was Sal and he said, "You caught me, you son of a gun." But he wasn't very upset.*
>
> *What a great guy Maglie was. He had been up with the Giants before I got there, and then he bounced all around, went to Mexico*

to play, and when he came back (in 1950), he was a different pitcher. He used to say "I'm going to make home plate mine," and he did. If a hitter was crowding the plate, he'd straighten him up. Sal was never scared to pitch inside. He was always ahead of the hitters, and he had great stuff.

Jansen came to the Giants in 1947, just a few months before his 27th birthday. He was old for a rookie and concerned with supporting a growing family that would eventually include 10 children. He knew time was running out on him:

> *The Giants weren't throwing money around in those days. When they brought me up, they paid me less than I was making in the Pacific Coast League. I asked for more money, but they said I had to win some games before they would give me a raise.*
>
> *I had been hit in the face in spring training, so I got a late start that season. And then the Giants put me in the bullpen. I had never pitched in relief in my life. It was getting close to cut-down time and I was worried that they were going to send me down. About five days before the cut-down date, I started against the Braves and beat them 2–1, and then I was in the rotation.*

The wins kept coming, 10 straight, and again Jansen asked for more money.

"The Giants gave me a $5,000 raise."

He finished the season 21–5 with 20 complete games, and would win 96 games in his first five seasons, topped off by his 23–11 record in 1951.

After his playing days were over, Jansen served as pitching coach for the Giants from 1961–71, and had a profound influence on two young pitchers, Juan Marichal and Gaylord Perry, both Hall of Famers.

"I didn't have to do a thing with Juan," he said. "There was nothing wrong with him. He had it all. Gaylord was a little different. In the beginning, his pitches were always high, high, high. All I did was get him to bend over when he threw and to concentrate on his catcher's target. He did the rest."

The "rest" included all that fidgeting on the mound, touching all parts of his body and his uniform before delivering the pitch, and, allegedly, loading up the baseball from time to time.

> Did Jansen know about the wet one?
>
> "Oh, yeah," he said sheepishly.
>
> Did he teach him that pitch?
>
> Jansen wouldn't say he did, but he wouldn't say he didn't, either.

Maglie and Jansen were good friends, but they also were both very competitive and they had a little friendly wager on which would win the most games that year. That rivalry pushed each of them and the Giants were the beneficiaries of that rivalry.

For most of that season, they were neck-and-neck in wins. On July 7, they were tied with 12 wins each, and they stayed neck-and-neck through July, August, and most of September. On September 23, Maglie beat the Braves, 4–1, for his 22nd win, two more than Jansen with only five games left in the regular season. Three days later, Jansen beat the Phillies, 10–1, but he would have only one more start, so when Maglie shut out the Braves, 3–0, on the next-to-last day of the season, it looked like he was a cinch to win their bet.

Jansen pitched the final game and beat the Braves, 3–2, a huge win because it assured the Giants of no worse than a tie for the pennant. But as luck would have it as far as Maglie and Jansen's bet was concerned, the Dodgers also won, setting up the three-game playoff.

Neither was ready to start in the first two games of the playoff and Maglie started the third game, so it seemed he would finish with more wins than Jansen. Maglie left after eight innings, trailing, 4–1, and Jansen came in to pitch the top of the ninth. The Dodgers were very good at getting on the other team. They were tough, and they were really letting Jansen have it. I can still hear them razzing him:

"Hey, Larry, where are you going to be pitching tomorrow?"

Jansen put the Dodgers down in order in the top of the ninth, but he still needed a miracle, and a miracle is what he got.

When we scored four runs in the bottom of the ninth to win, 5–4, Jansen was the pitcher of record, his 23rd win, tied with Maglie for the league lead to win their bet.

Jansen was released by the Giants midway through the 1954 season, missing out on a chance to pitch in another World Series. He went back to his home in the northwest and was a pitcher/coach for Seattle in the Pacific Coast

Larry Jansen, the runner-up to Jackie Robinson in Rookie of the Year voting in 1947, later played a huge role in the development of future Hall of Famers Juan Marichal and Gaylord Perry. *Photo courtesy of Diamond Images/Getty Images.*

League. The Reds gave him a chance in 1956. He won two games for them, lost three, and retired with a career record of 122 89.

Later the Giants brought Larry back as pitching coach, and he was instrumental in the development of Juan Marichal and Gaylord Perry, numbers two and three on my list of all-time Giants right-handed pitchers and both members of the Hall of Fame.

Statistical Summaries

All statistics are from player's Giants career only.

PITCHING

G = Games
W = Games won
L = Games lost
PCT = Winning percentage
SHO = Shutouts
SO = Strikeouts
ERA = Earned run average

Right-Handed Pitcher	Years	G	W	L	PCT	SHO	SO	ERA
Christy Mathewson *Stole home on September 12, 1911*	1900–16	634	372	188	.664	79	2,499	2.12
Juan Marichal *Struck out seven consecutive Philadelphia batters on September 4, 1964*	1960–73	458	238	140	.630	52	2,281	2.84

continued	Years	G	W	L	PCT	SHO	SO	ERA
Gaylord Perry *Had 12 complete game 1–0 victories during his career*	1962–71	367	134	109	.551	21	1,606	2.96
Sal Maglie *Had 11 consecutive victories during the 1950 season*	1945 1950–55	221	95	42	.693	20	654	3.13
Larry Jansen *Pitched five scoreless innings with six strikeouts in the 1950 All-Star Game*	1947–54	283	120	86	.583	17	826	3.55

FIELDING

PO = Putouts

A = Assists

E = Errors

DP = Double plays

TC/G = Total chances divided by games played

FA = Fielding average

Right-Handed Pitcher	PO	A	E	DP	TC/G	FA
Christy Mathewson	280	1,500	52	41	2.8	.972
Juan Marichal	287	567	47	27	2.0	.948
Gaylord Perry	173	424	17	27	1.9	.972
Sal Maglie	70	232	8	20	1.4	.974
Larry Jansen	135	331	11	31	1.7	.977

TEN

Left-Handed Pitcher

By the time I got to the Giants, **Carl Hubbell** was three years into retirement as a player and was working in the team's front office as director of minor league operations. I had heard that it was Hubbell who told general manager Bill Terry "this kid should be playing someplace," when I wasn't playing very much in Bristol, Virginia, and that's when I was moved to Rocky Mount, North Carolina, and got a chance to play.

I got to know Hubbell a little, but not very well, after I went up to the Giants, but I never had a chance to ask him if that story was true. I remember Hubbell as a tall, very thin fellow, and a very nice man. I couldn't help but notice his crooked arm, probably from all those years of throwing the screwball.

1. CARL HUBBELL

2. RUBE MARQUARD

3. ART NEHF

4. JOHNNY ANTONELLI

5. BILLY PIERCE

Of course, growing up a Giants fan, I knew about Hubbell as a pitcher, one of the great names in Giants history. Everybody knows about what Hubbell did in the second All-Star Game ever played, in 1934 in the Polo Grounds. I was 12 years old at the time and I really don't remember it, but I certainly have heard and read a lot about what he did. Everybody has.

Hubbell started that game for the National League against Lefty Gomez of the Yankees. In the top of the first inning, Charlie Gehringer led off with a single and Hubbell walked Heinie Manush. Now he had to face Babe Ruth, Lou Gehrig, and Jimmie Foxx, three of the greatest sluggers the game has known (they would combine to hit 115 homers among them that season), with two on and nobody out.

Well, Hubbell struck out Ruth looking at a screwball. Then he struck out Gehrig swinging on four pitches and struck out Foxx on three screwballs.

In the second inning, he struck out Al Simmons and Joe Cronin. He had struck out five consecutive hitters, all of whom would make the Hall of Fame. It's more than 70 years later, and people still talk about that performance by Hubbell.

Although the 1934 All-Star Game was Hubbell's shining hour in baseball, don't get the idea he was just a one-game wonder. He was much more than that. He had a remarkable, brilliant career, 16 major league seasons, all of them with the Giants.

Hubbell started his career with Oklahoma City in the Western League. The Detroit Tigers purchased his contract in 1925, but Hubbell was mostly disappointing in the Tigers' farm system. When he got a chance to go to spring training with the Tigers, manager Ty Cobb forbade Hubbell to throw his signature pitch, the screwball, and sent him back to the minor leagues.

A Giants scout convinced John McGraw to acquire him and McGraw encouraged Hubbell to throw his screwball. The rest, as they say, is history. And what history!

In 1928, his rookie season, Hubbell won 10 games. The next year, he won 18. Soon, he was the ace of the Giants pitching staff.

In 1933, he led the National League with 23 wins, an earned-run average of 1.66, 308⅔ innings, and 10 shutouts, and was named Most Valuable Player in the league. He followed that up by winning two games in the World Series against Washington, not allowing an earned run in 20 innings.

Hubbell went on to win 20 games or more in each of the next four seasons and helped pitch the Giants to National League pennants in 1936 and '37. In 1936, Hubbell led the league in wins with 26, winning percentage with .813 and earned-run average with 2.31, and won his second MVP award, making him the only pitcher ever to win two MVPs during peace time (Hal Newhouser won two in 1944 and '45 when the talent pool was diluted by World War II).

Carl Hubbell spent his entire 16-year career pitching for the Giants, compiling a 253–154 record as well as a brilliant strikeout-to-walk ratio.

More than 70 years later, it's still the greatest performance in the history of baseball's annual All-Star Game, "King" Carl Hubbell, the "Meal Ticket" of the New York Giants, striking out five future Hall of Famers in succession.

Here, in Hubbell's own words, are his remembrances of that magical afternoon in the Polo Grounds as told many years later to Chicago columnist John Carmichael:

As far as control and stuff is concerned, I never had any more in my life than for that game. I can remember Frankie Frisch coming off the field behind me at the end of the third inning, grunting to Bill Terry, "I could play second base 15 more years behind that guy. He doesn't need any help. He does it all by himself."

Then we hit the bench, and Terry slapped me on the arm and said, "That's pitching, boy," and Gabby Hartnett let his mask fall down and yelled at the American League dugout, "We gotta look at that all season," and I was pretty happy.

But I never was a strikeout pitcher like Bob Feller or Dizzy Dean or Dazzy Vance. My style of pitching was to make the other team hit the ball, but on the ground. It was as big a surprise to me to strike out all those fellows as it probably was to them. Before the game, Gabby Hartnett and I went down the lineup: Charlie Gehringer, Heinie Manush, Babe Ruth, Lou Gehrig, Jimmie Foxx, Al Simmons, Joe Cronin, Bill Dickey, and Lefty Gomez. There probably wasn't a pitcher they'd ever faced that they hadn't belted one off him somewhere, sometime. We couldn't discuss weaknesses...they didn't have any, except Gomez. Finally, Gabby said, "We'll waste everything except the screwball. Get that over, but keep your fastball and hook outside. We can't let 'em hit it in the air." So that's the way we started. I knew I had only three innings to work and could bear down on every pitch.

They talk about those All-Star Games being exhibition affairs, and maybe they are, but I've seen very few players in my life who didn't want to win, no matter whom they were playing or what for. If I'm playing cards for pennies, I want to win. How can you feel any other way? Besides, there were 50,000 fans or more there, and they wanted to see the best you've got. There was an obligation to the people, as well as to ourselves, to go all out. I can recall walking out to the hill in the Polo Grounds that day and looking around the stands and thinking to myself, "Hub, they want to see what you've got."

Gehringer was first up and Hartnett called for a waste ball just so I'd get the feel of the first pitch. It was a little too close and Charlie singled. Down from one of the stands came a yell, "Take him out!" I had to laugh. Terry took a couple of steps off first and hollered, "That's all right," and there was Manush at the plate. If I recollect rightly, I got two strikes on him, but then he refused to swing any more, and I lost him. He walked. This time Terry and Frankie Frisch and Pie Traynor and Travis Jackson all came over to the mound and began worrying. "Are you all right?" Bill asked me. I assured him I was. I could hear more than one voice from the stands, "Take him out before it's too late."

Well, I could imagine how they felt with two on, nobody out, and Ruth at bat. To strike him out was the last thought in my mind. The thing was to make him hit on the ground. He wasn't too fast, as you know, and he'd be a cinch to double. He never took the bat off his shoulder. You could have pushed me over with your little finger. I fed him three straight screwballs, all over the plate, after wasting a fastball, and he stood there. I can see him looking at the umpire on "You're out," and he wasn't mad. He just didn't believe it, and Hartnett was laughing when he threw the ball back.

So up came Gehrig. He was a sharp hitter. You could double him, too, now and then, if the ball was hit hard and straight at an infielder. That's what we hoped he'd do, at best. Striking out Ruth and Gehrig in succession was too big an order. But, by golly, he fanned...and on four pitches. He swung at the last screwball, and you should have heard that crowd. I felt a lot easier then, and even when Gehringer and Manush pulled a double steal and got to second and third, with Foxx up, I looked down at Hartnett and caught the screwball sign, and Jimmie missed. We were really trying to strike Foxx out, with two already gone, and Gabby didn't bother to waste any pitches. I threw three more screwballs, and he went down swinging. We had set down the side on 12 pitches, and then Frisch hit a homer in our half of the first, and we were ahead.

It was funny, when I thought of it afterward, how Ruth and Gehrig looked as they stood there. The Babe must have been waiting for me to get the ball up a little so he could get his bat under it. He always was trying for that one big shot at the stands, and anything around his knees, especially a twisting ball, didn't let him get any leverage. Gehrig apparently decided to take one swing at least, and he beat down at the pitch, figuring to take a chance on being doubled up if he could get a piece of the ball. He whispered something to Foxx as Jim got up from the batter's circle, and while I didn't hear it, I found out later he said, "You might as well cut. It won't get any higher."

That season, Hubbell was 10–6 on July 17 when he went on a streak and won his last 16 decisions. And then he followed that up by winning his first eight decisions in 1937 for a 24-game winning streak that still stands as a major league record.

Three things in Hubbell's career stand out as a sign of his times. In 1934, he not only won 21 games, he was credited with a league-leading eight saves; four times he pitched more than 300 innings; and on July 2, 1933, he pitched a complete game, 18-inning 1–0 victory over the Cardinals, striking out 12 and walking none.

When he retired after the 1943 season, Hubbell had a record of 253–154, a winning percentage of .622 and a tremendous strikeout-to-walk ratio of 1,678-724, or 2.3-to-1.

Four years after he retired, Hubbell was elected to the Hall of Fame.

Rube Marquard won 201 major league games, 73 of them in a three-year period from 1911–13, pitched a no-hitter, won a record 19 consecutive games in 1912, and was elected to the Hall of Fame.

Not bad for a pitcher who, early in his career, was known as "the $11,000 lemon."

When Marquard won 20 games for Indianapolis in 1908, John McGraw, with his eye for talent, signed him for the Giants to a then-record contract worth $11,000. On September 25 in the Polo Grounds, Marquard made his major league debut. He hit the first batter, walked the next two, and all three scored. Marquard was removed from the game after the fifth inning, and as he walked to the center-field clubhouse, bleacher fans serenaded him with the "$11,000 lemon" tag.

Three years later, the fans were singing a different tune.

In 1911, Marquard won 24 games, combined with Christy Mathewson for 50 victories, and helped pitch the Giants to their first of three consecutive National League pennants.

The 1912 season was Marquard's best. He led the league with 26 wins (Mathewson won 23), won 19 straight games (he didn't lose until July 3), and won two more games in the World Series against Boston.

Born Richard William Marquard, the 6'3", 180-pound left-hander, got the nickname "Rube" from a newspaper story that compared him to Rube Waddell, at the time the American League strikeout king.

Rube Marquard, who was once considered a bust, won a record 19 straight games during the 1912 season in the heyday of his Hall of Fame career. *Photo courtesy of MLB Photos via Getty Images.*

"He is so tall and skinny," read the account, "he looks like a big number one when he stands on the mound, but he pitches like Rube Waddell."

From that day forward, Marquard was called "Rube."

In his heyday, Marquard was a bon vivant, multi-faceted, man-about-town. After his outstanding 1912 season, he was deluged with show business offers. He appeared in a movie, *19 Straight*, and hit the vaudeville circuit teamed with Blossom Seeley, then the reigning queen of vaudeville, and later married her.

Marquard won 23 games in 1913 (Mathewson won 25) and the Giants won their third straight pennant, but then his career began to nose-dive. He slipped to 12–22 in 1914 and was 9–8 in 1915 when, with John McGraw's permission, he arranged his own sale to, of all teams, the Dodgers for $7,500. He enjoyed a brief resurgence in Brooklyn, winning 13 games in 1916 and 19 in 1917, and pitching in two more World Series with the Dodgers.

After the 1920 season, he was traded to Cincinnati, where he won 17 games and then was traded to the Braves. A series of injuries and illnesses caused his career to spiral downward in Boston. He won only 25 games in four seasons with the Braves and then retired.

In retirement, Marquard became a jack-of-all-trades. He managed in the minor leagues without much success, tried umpiring, was a scout and coach for Atlanta in the Southern Association, and for years worked as a mutual clerk at racetracks in Florida and Maryland.

Marquard lived to the ripe old age of 90. He died in 1980, nine years after being elected to the Hall of Fame.

What the Yankees are today—the best team money can buy—the Giants were in John McGraw's day. They were baseball's most successful and wealthiest team in the first quarter of the 20th century and they used their resources to swoop in and purchase outstanding players from teams in need of money.

On August 15, 1919, with the Giants in second place, seven games behind Cincinnati, McGraw made a deal designed to overtake the Reds. He sent four players plus $55,000, a hefty sum in those days, to the Braves for left-hander **Art Nehf,** who had won 32 games for the light hitting Braves in the previous two seasons.

Nehf won nine of 11 decisions, but the Giants were unable to catch the Reds and finished a well-beaten second. However, the trade would pay off

Art Nehf went 107–60 during seven outstanding seasons as the Giants' left-handed ace.
Photo courtesy of Bettmann/CORBIS.

in large measure for the Giants in the following years as Nehf became the ace of a pitching staff that helped the Giants win four consecutive pennants.

Nehf won 21 games, tops on the staff, in 1920, but again the Giants finished in second place, behind Brooklyn. The following year, Nehf again led the Giants in wins with 20 and helped pitch them into the World Series against the Yankees.

In the World Series, Nehf hooked up in three pitching gems with future Hall of Famer Waite Hoyt. In Game 2, Nehf allowed only three hits, but the Giants managed only two singles off Hoyt and the Yankees won, 3–0, to take a two games to none lead in the Series.

Nehf and Hoyt hooked up again four days later. Again, Hoyt prevailed, 3–1, despite being touched up for 10 hits, and the Yankees took a three games to two lead in what was then a best-of-nine World Series.

When the Giants won the next two games, it was Hoyt vs. Nehf again in Game 8. This time, Nehf got the upper hand. The Giants scored an unearned run in the top of the first and Nehf let that run stand up for a 1–0 victory and the Giants first world championship in 16 years.

Although he was 1–2 in the Series, Nehf allowed the Yankees only four earned runs and 13 hits in three games covering 26 innings. And he held Babe Ruth to just one hit, a bunt single, in six at-bats for the Series.

Nehf won 19 games in 1922 and led the Giants to another pennant and a rematch with the Yankees in the World Series. Nehf dueled Bullet Joe Bush in Game 1 and left after seven innings, with the Giants trailing, 2–0. A three-run rally in the eighth gave the Giants a 3–2 victory, but Nehf was not involved in the decision.

With the Giants ahead, three games to none (Game 2 ended in a tie), Nehf again opposed Bush in Game 5. For the second straight year, Nehf pitched and won the game that clinched the World Series for the Giants, a 5–3 victory. And for the second straight year, Nehf stymied the mighty Ruth, holding him to one hit, a single, in six at-bats.

In 1923 the Giants won their third straight pennant, and for the third straight year their World Series opponent was the Yankees, now in their own home—brand-new Yankee Stadium in the Bronx, across the Harlem River from the Polo Grounds. Although he slipped to a record of 13–10, Nehf got the start in Game 3 against Sam Jones.

With the Series tied one game each, Nehf put the Giants ahead with a 1–0 victory, the only run scored on a Casey Stengel home run in the seventh inning.

For the third straight year, Nehf pitched the decisive game of the Series, but this time he was on the losing end, 6–4, as the Yankees won their first of many World Series. Also at an end was Nehf's dominance of Ruth, who solved the Giants left-hander and blasted a tremendous home run in the first inning, his third homer of the Series.

Nehf was 14–4 in 1924 as the Giants won their fourth straight pennant, but this time they didn't have to contend with their intercity rivals. The Washington Senators won the American League pennant and opposed the Giants in the World Series.

Nehf got the start in Game 1 and dueled the great Walter Johnson to a 2–2 tie through 11 innings. The Giants scored two in the top of the twelfth, but the Senators came back with an unearned run in the bottom of the twelfth and had the tying run on third with two outs when Nehf retired Goose Goslin on a smash to first baseman George Kelly to give the Giants a 4–3 victory.

With a chance to pitch the World Series clincher for the third time in four years, Nehf lost Game 6, 2–1, to Tom Zachary and the Senators then won Game 7 and the Series.

On the decline, Nehf was 11–9 for the Giants in 1925 and after pitching two games without a decision in 1926, he was sold to the Reds. In seven seasons with the Giants, he won 107 games and lost only 60.

With the Reds, Nehf pitched infrequently. He was released in 1927 and signed with the Cubs, with whom he had a brief resurgence in 1928 when he won 13 games and lost seven. The following year, he would get one more chance to pitch in the World Series when the Cubs faced the Philadelphia Athletics.

Nehf entered Game 4 in the seventh inning with the Athletics in the midst of a 10-run rally. Mule Haas greeted him with a three-run homer. After Mickey Cochrane drew a walk, Nehf was replaced by Sheriff Blake and never pitched another game.

It's not often that you're traded for a guy and then a couple of years later, you not only become his teammate, but also his roommate. That's the kind of thing that can happen in baseball, and it happened to me.

A few weeks before the start of spring training in 1954, the Giants sent a catcher named Sam Calderone and me to the Milwaukee Braves for four players and $50,000.

(As an aside, and in keeping with the idea that baseball makes strange bed-fellows, in Milwaukee my roommate was Andy Pafko, who had been the Dodgers left fielder in the third game of the 1951 playoff and over whose head the game-winning home run I hit sailed.)

One of the four players the Giants got back from Milwaukee in that trade was left-hander **Johnny Antonelli,** who was one of baseball's first bonus babies. He had signed with the Boston Braves in 1948 for a bonus of $65,000, but in four years with the Braves in Boston and Milwaukee, he had won only 17 games and lost 22, and I was coming off a year in which I batted .288, hit 26 home runs, and drove in 106 runs. As a result, the Giants were rather severely criticized for the trade.

I was sent to Milwaukee as part of the trade that landed Johnny Antonelli in New York, where he proceeded to win 21 games in his first season and lead a World Series sweep of the Indians. *Photo courtesy of Time Life Pictures/Getty Images.*

It didn't take long for Antonelli to win over Giants fans. He won 21 games in his first year with the Giants, beat the Indians, 3–1, in Game 2 of the World Series, and then came back in relief with an inning and two-thirds to save Game 4 that nailed down the sweep. Meanwhile, I had broken my foot in spring training and played in only 43 games, so the Giants got the best of that trade.

And they continued to profit from the trade when Antonelli won 14 and 20 games the next two years.

In June of 1957, the Giants got me back from the Braves, which didn't make me very happy because I was with a pretty good team in Milwaukee. But I went back with the Giants and that's how I wound up being Antonelli's roommate. John was having a terrible year, but I don't think it was my fault. I wasn't there in his first three years with the Giants when he won 55 games, so I can't say what happened to him in '57. It just seemed to me that something was going on in his head; he had lost his confidence, or something.

In any case, Antonelli was 12–18 that season, and he also may have helped get me traded again. One day, Johnny and I were late getting to the ballpark in Pittsburgh. We had been out late the night before having dinner and we both overslept, so we got to the ballpark late. And when we walked into the locker room, I could see on manager Bill Rigney's face that he wasn't very pleased.

The next year the Giants moved to San Francisco. I went to spring training, expecting to go with the Giants to the West Coast, but about a week before the season, I was traded to the Cubs, so I never got to play in San Francisco as a Giant.

After I left, Antonelli had two more good years. He won 16 games in 1958 and 19 in 1959, so maybe his one-year slump was my fault.

I see John every once in awhile at some baseball function, and when I do, I never fail to blame him for getting me traded from the Giants to the Cubs because it was his fault we showed up late that day in Pittsburgh.

I'm making **Billy Pierce** number five on my list of left-handed pitchers for the Giants mainly because of his great body of work: 211 victories, including back-to-back 20-win seasons, with three teams, the Tigers, White Sox, and Giants. He won only 22 games with the Giants, but he was a big reason the Giants got to the World Series in 1962, a season that reawakened memories of 1951.

Eleven years later and 3,000 miles away, the Giants and Dodgers ended the season tied for first place when, just as they had in 1951, the Dodgers had taken a big lead in midseason and blew it.

Once again, these two archrivals met in a three-game playoff. Game 1 was played in Candlestick Park, with Pierce pitching against Sandy Koufax. The Giants knocked Koufax out in the second inning and won, 8–0, behind Pierce's complete game three-hitter.

The Dodgers came back to win Game 2, just as they had done 11 years earlier, this time by an 8–7 score, and once again they came down to a sudden-death third game. Déjà vu all over again, as Yogi Berra would say, with Juan Marichal starting against Johnny Podres.

And the third game in 1962 was eerily similar to the third game of the 1951 playoff, with the Dodgers taking a 4–2 lead into the ninth inning. Sound familiar?

By winning the final game of the playoff and Game 6 of the 1962 World Series, Pierce had done enough to pitch himself into Giants lore.

Billy Pierce won only 22 games as a Giant, but he was instrumental in getting us to the 1962 World Series. *Photo courtesy of the National Baseball Hall of Fame.*

Well, the familiarity doesn't stop there, because the Giants rallied for four runs in the ninth, just like in '51. Only this time the Dodgers were the home team and the four runs didn't win the game. The Giants still had to hold the Dodgers in the bottom of the ninth and to do so, manager Alvin Dark called on Pierce to protect the lead in relief. Billy did it with ease, setting the Dodgers down 1-2-3 for a save in the 6–4 victory that won the pennant.

In the World Series against the Yankees, Pierce got the start in Game 3. He pitched well enough to win, but was beaten, 3–2. But Pierce came back in the sixth game, pitched a complete game, held the Yankees to three hits, and beat them, 5–2, to send the Series to a seventh game.

The Yankees won that seventh game, and the World Series, 1–0. But by winning the final game of the playoff and Game 6 of the World Series, Pierce had done enough to pitch himself into Giants lore, and onto my all-time Giants team.

Statistical Summaries

All statistics are from player's Giants career only.

PITCHING

G = Games

W = Games won

L = Games lost

PCT = Winning percentage

SHO = Shutouts

SO = Strikeouts

ERA = Earned run average

Left-Handed Pitcher	Years	G	W	L	PCT	SHO	SO	ERA
Carl Hubbell *Completed 60 percent of his career starts (260/431)*	1928–43	535	253	154	.622	36	1677	2.98
Rube Marquard *Pitched 21 innings to beat Pittsburgh on May 17, 1914*	1908–15	239	103	76	.575	16	897	2.85
Art Nehf *Hit two home runs against St. Louis on July 29, 1924*	1919–26	226	107	60	.641	12	415	3.45

continued	Years	G	W	L	PCT	SHO	SO	ERA
Johnny Antonelli *Winning pitcher in first of two All Star Games played in 1959*	1954–60	280	108	84	.562	21	919	3.13
Billy Pierce *Finished third in Cy Young Award voting behind Don Drysdale and Jack Sanford in 1962*	1962–64	102	22	17	.564	3	157	3.54

FIELDING

PO = Putouts

A = Assists

E = Errors

DP = Double plays

TC/G = Total chances divided by games played

FA = Fielding average

Left-Handed Pitcher	PO	A	E	DP	TC/G	FA
Carl Hubbell	155	824	33	55	1.9	.967
Rube Marquard	26	335	22	7	1.6	.943
Art Nehf	81	389	11	32	2.1	.977
Johnny Antonelli	57	266	14	22	1.2	.958
Billy Pierce	9	51	2	5	0.6	.968

ELEVEN

Relief Pitcher

The game of baseball has changed so much that if you talk today about **Hoyt Wilhelm** being a great relief pitcher people will laugh at you because he saved 20 games in a season just three times and had only 227 saves in a 21-year career. Those are puny numbers compared to what relievers, or closers, are doing nowadays.

Wilhelm pitched most of his career at a time when saves weren't an official statistic of baseball. They were not listed among a pitcher's statistics so there was very little incentive for a reliever to pile up big numbers of saves.

It wasn't until 1969 that baseball adopted an official saves rule and that's when saves began to show up among the statistics. In order to update the pitching records of relievers throughout the history of baseball, statisticians

1. HOYT WILHELM

2. STU MILLER

3. MARV GRISSOM

4. ROBB NEN

5. ROD BECK

scoured thousands of box scores dating all the way back to 1876 and computed the number of saves for all pitchers.

The save rule underwent several changes until baseball arrived at the current formula, which credits a save for any pitcher who protects a lead for at least three innings, or enters the game with the tying run on deck.

It wasn't until the 1980s that saves became prominent and the relief pitcher began to earn the recognition, and the pay, that had eluded them for the game's first 100 years. Today, relief pitchers are accorded superstar status. They are considered as important to a team's success as a starting pitcher and they are paid accordingly (Mariano Rivera of the Yankees, for example, earns more than $10 million annually).

Wilhelm was one of the first great relief pitchers, the best of his time, the 1950s and 1960s, with that baffling, tantalizing knuckleball of his. He had the best knuckleball I've ever seen. He was the most consistent with it. He threw more strikes with the knuckleball than anybody I've ever seen. He could really break that ball. It would be all over the place.

Hoyt was a pioneer, the first relief pitcher elected to the Hall of Fame. He won 124 games in relief, a major league record. He even started 52 games, completed 20 of them, and pitched a no-hitter for Baltimore against the Yankees in 1958.

But it was in relief that Wilhelm excelled, and it was as a relief pitcher that he came to the Giants in 1952, at the advanced age of 28. He had lost three years in the army and had been a war hero during World War II. He was awarded the Purple Heart for bravery during the Battle of the Bulge.

Hoyt stayed five years with the Giants, pitching exclusively in relief. He saved only 41 games in those five years, but he won 42. (The career record for saves is 482 by Trevor Hoffman, and the single-season saves record is 57 by Bobby Thigpen of the Chicago White Sox in 1990.)

Relief pitchers were used differently in those days, often pitching two, three, and even four innings. In his five years as a Giant, Wilhelm appeared in 319 games and pitched 608 innings, which averages out to a little less than two innings per appearance.

When he slumped in the 1955 and 1956 seasons, Wilhelm was traded to the Cardinals. He was 34 at the time, and a lot of people figured he was at the end of the line. But his best years were still ahead of him.

He would pitch 16 more seasons, finally retiring at the age of 49 having pitched in more games than any other pitcher, 1,070. He also had pitched more games in relief (1,018), finished more games (651), and pitched more relief innings (1,870) than any other pitcher.

It was in 1960, while Wilhelm was pitching for Baltimore, that Orioles manager Paul Richards designed the oversized mitt to help his frustrated catchers hold on to Hoyt's elusive knuckleball, a practice still in use today.

Hoyt Wilhelm was a pioneer and the first true relief pitcher elected to baseball's Hall of Fame; though, in comparison, his numbers are dwarfed by those of today's "closers."

*T*hey are kindred spirits, birds of a feather, a small, but exclusive club with a strong bond. They are knuckleball pitchers, the rarest of the rare in baseball.

Only two pitchers who have used the knuckleball as their primary pitch have been elected to the Hall of Fame. They are Hoyt Wilhelm and Phil Niekro.

Between them they pitched in the major leagues for 45 years, appeared in 1,934 games, worked 7,658 innings, contributed 718 victories (461 wins, 257 saves), and struck out 4,952 batters, most of them with that tantalizing, baffling, elusive knuckleball.

"My father taught me to throw the knuckleball when I was in grade school," said Niekro, who years later would pick up the nickname "Knucksie." "I threw it all through high school and when I was 18, the Braves signed me for $500."

Niekro's advancement was retarded by skepticism over the pitch that was rare and difficult to control. He finally broke into the big leagues with 10 games in 1964 for the Braves, then in Milwaukee. At the time, Wilhelm was 42 years old and a veteran of 12 major league seasons.

Because Wilhelm was in the American League and Niekro was in the National, they rarely crossed paths, except in spring training. When they did, Niekro never failed to take advantage of the opportunity.

"He was the only guy I could go to at the time," Niekro said. "Later, there was Charlie Hough, Wilbur Wood, and my brother, Joe, but back then, there was only Hoyt, and he was the best. He's the greatest knuckleball pitcher of all time, and he always will be."

By 1969, the Braves had moved to Atlanta and Niekro was their ace pitcher when the fates conspired to put Niekro and Wilhelm on the same team. On September 8, 1969, the Braves, looking for veteran bullpen help, acquired Wilhelm and pitcher Bob Priddy from the California Angels in exchange for Mickey Rivers and Clint Compton.

Twenty-two days later, needing one win to clinch the National League West championship, the Braves sent 22-game winner Niekro to the mound against the Cincinnati Reds in Atlanta. Trailing, 2–1, the Braves rallied for two runs in the bottom of the seventh to take a 3–2 lead.

With Niekro having been removed for a pinch-hitter in the two-run rally, Wilhelm entered to pitch the eighth. Bobby Tolan tried to bunt his way on and was thrown out by catcher Bob Didier. Wilhelm then struck out Tony Perez and Johnny Bench.

In the ninth, Wilhelm again retired the Reds in order on a strikeout, a fly ball to right, and a ground out to short, and the Braves were NL West champions.

Niekro got the win, his 23rd, two behind league leader Tom Seaver. Wilhelm picked up the save. He was 47 years old at the time.

Niekro and Wilhelm would remain teammates until the following September when Wilhelm was sold to the Cubs. In their time together, they bonded and became close friends and fishing buddies. And they often talked pitching, of course.

Of their relationship, Niekro said:

> There aren't too many pitching coaches who know about the knuckleball, so those of us who threw the knuckleball had to be our own coaches, or each other's coaches. And who better to talk to about the knuckleball then Hoyt? We'd talk about grips and spins and releases. I got a lot out of talking to him. He was a big influence on me. No two knuckleball pitchers are alike, but Hoyt and I were very similar in the way we gripped the ball and released it. He threw his a lot more than I did, and he had better control of it than I did, but we were similar and he helped me quite a bit.
>
> I met Dutch Leonard [a famed knuckleballer who won 20 games for the Washington Senators in 1939], but I never saw him pitch and I didn't get to talk with him too much. Hoyt Wilhelm was my guru.

Like most pitchers of his era, before relief pitchers became prominent, **Stu Miller** started his career as a starter with the Cardinals. He wasn't a very big guy and not very impressive looking, just 5'11", 165 pounds, and when his manager, the acerbic Eddie Stanky, saw him his comment was, "Who's that stenographer?"

Nevertheless, the "stenographer" broke in with a splash, shutting out the Cubs, 1–0, in his major league debut and following that up by holding the Dodgers hitless into the eighth inning in his fourth major league start.

I hit against Miller and, believe me, it was no picnic. He didn't throw hard, but he would throw a lot of junk up there and he could drive you nuts with his change of speeds. He'd throw curveballs at several speeds, all slow, and he even changed speeds on his change-up. To make him even tougher, he had a herky-jerk delivery that would mess up a hitter's timing. Sometimes he'd go into his wind-up and just before he was ready to deliver the ball, he'd come to a complete stop, hesitate, and then throw. I'm telling you, he could make a hitter crazy.

After a 6–3 record in his rookie season, Miller struggled and bounced around. He was traded to the Phillies in 1956 and to the Giants a year later.

It was with the Giants in San Francisco that Miller became a reliever, one of the best of his time, and also where he experienced his signature moment during the 1961 All-Star Game.

In 1958, splitting his time between starting and relieving, Miller led the National League in earned-run average with 2.47, but he still did not have a winning record. By 1959, he was being used almost exclusively in relief, closing out games, but baseball still had not begun to use closers like they do today and that season Miller won seven games in relief and saved eight others (the league leaders in saves, Don McMahon of the Braves and Lindy McDaniel of the Cardinals, had only 15).

By 1961, Miller was being used exclusively in relief by the Giants. He appeared in 63 games, led the league in relief wins with 14 and saves with 17, was named National League Fireman of the Year, and was selected for the All-Star team.

They used to say that Miller had three speeds—slow, slower, and slowest and that he threw a pitch that stopped…To make him even tougher, he had a herky-jerk delivery that would mess up a hitter's timing.

That was the time baseball experimented with two All-Star Games and the first one was played in Candlestick Park, known for the ferocious winds that would kick up every afternoon, usually about 3:00. It was because of the wind that so many players hated playing there. Miller, in particular, was troubled by the wind because he wasn't very big and he could easily be blown away by a stiff wind, which is exactly what happened in the All-Star Game on the afternoon of July 11, 1961.

As the top of the ninth started, with the National League leading, 3–1, the wind began to kick up. With one out, Norm Cash doubled and Al Kaline followed with an RBI single to make it 3–2. When Roger Maris singled off Sandy Koufax to move Kaline to second, Miller was brought in to face Rocky Colavito.

Now the wind was really kicking up a storm and as Miller began to pitch to Colavito, the wind blew him right off the mound. He was charged with a balk, the runners moving up to second and third. Kaline scored the tying

Stu Miller (center), flanked by Don Larsen (left) and Bobby Bolin, became a relief specialist who drove hitters crazy with his arsenal of off-speed pitches.

run on an error by third baseman Ken Boyer, and there was a wind-blown foul pop dropped by catcher Smokey Burgess and an error by Don Zimmer before Miller got out of the inning by retiring Hoyt Wilhelm.

In the top of the tenth, the American League grabbed the lead against Miller on an unearned run because of another error by Boyer. The wind was wreaking havoc not only on Miller, but also on the fielders. Stu struck out Maris to end the inning and became the winning pitcher when the National League scored two in the bottom of the tenth on a single by Hank Aaron, a passed ball, an RBI double by Mays, and a game-winning single by Roberto Clemente.

A year later, the Giants traded Miller to Baltimore, where he continued to be a dominant reliever. In his first three seasons with the Orioles, he saved 74 games, which may not seem like many by today's standards, but he led the American League in saves in 1963, was third in 1964, and tied for second in 1965.

Marv Grissom is another relief pitcher whose statistics don't provide a true picture of how dominant he was because he pitched in the era before relievers became the specialists they are today.

Like Stu Miller, and so many others in the 1950s, Grissom began his career as a starting pitcher, but had only moderate success with the Giants, Tigers, White Sox, and Red Sox, winning 16 and losing 22.

The Giants got him back midway through 1953, when Marv was 35, and used him mostly in relief. The next year, he became their stopper, winning nine games in relief and saving 19, and then closing out Game 1 of the World Series against the Indians with two and two-thirds scoreless innings to get the win.

Marv stayed with the Giants through 1958, winning 17 more games in relief and saving 39 others. But by then he was 40 years old and the Giants had decided to turn the relief job over to Stu Miller.

Grissom was a big, tough-looking guy, 6'3", 190 pounds, who looked like the Marlboro Man. If he wasn't a baseball player, I could see him making it big as a movie cowboy. He sure looked the part.

This is all you need to know to understand how the role of the relief pitcher, or closer, has changed in baseball over the last 50 years:

- In five years with the Giants, Hoyt Wilhelm, pitching mainly in relief and occasionally as a starter, had 42 relief wins and 41 saves, and

Marv Grissom was a more imposing figure on the mound than Stu Miller, who succeeded him as the Giants' main relief pitcher, but like all the guys who filled this role in the 1950s and 1960s, Grissom's numbers don't tell the whole story. *Photo courtesy of Bettmann/CORBIS.*

pitched 607 innings in 319 games, an average of 1.9 innings per appearance. Four times he pitched more than 100 innings, with a high of 159⅓.

• In six years with the Giants, Stu Miller, who also started occasionally, had 37 relief wins and 47 saves, and pitched 804 innings in 307

Robb Nen averaged 41 saves per season with the Giants, including a league-leading 45 in 2001.

games, an average of 2.6 innings per appearance. He never pitched fewer than 100 innings in any of those six seasons, with a high of 182 innings.

- In five and a half seasons with the Giants, Marv Grissom, who also started on occasion, had 26 wins in relief and 58 saves, and pitched 543 innings in 285 appearances, or 1.9 innings per appearance, with a high of 122 innings.
- In five years with the Giants, **Robb Nen,** who never started a game, had 24 wins and 206 saves, and pitched 379 innings in 365 games, or just a bit over one inning per appearance. He never pitched more than 88⅔ innings in any of those five seasons.

Nen's 206 saves are a record for the Giants, in New York or San Francisco, but does that mean he was a better relief pitcher than Wilhelm, Miller, or Grissom? I don't think so. It's simply that the role of the relief pitcher has changed dramatically in the past half century.

Had they been pitching today when closers often entered a game in the ninth inning with a lead of three runs or fewer and nobody on base, I have no doubt that Wilhelm, Miller, and Grissom all would have averaged 41 saves a season, as Nen did, and more.

The same might be said for other Giants relievers like Ace Adams, Bob Shaw, Frank Linzy, Don McMahon, and Randy Moffitt. Each of them pitched all, or most, of their careers prior to 1980, when the role of the reliever started to change.

I mean to take nothing away from Nen, or others of his era. In the five years he spent as a Giant, Nen, whose dad, Dick, had been a first baseman with the Dodgers, Cubs, and Senators, was a dominant closer. In 2001, he led the National League in saves with 45.

Don't blame Nen for coming along in an era when the role of relief pitchers changed and they became more prominent. It wasn't his doing. It's just that things changed in baseball, and Nen was good enough to profit from that change.

Everything that was said about Robb Nen also could be said about **Rod Beck,** whose career closely mirrors Nen's. He became the Giants' closer in 1992 and was second in the league in saves in three of the next five years.

Rod Beck, shown after closing out the NL West–clinching game in 1997, was the Giants' saves leader until Robb Nen succeeded and eventually surpassed him. *Photo courtesy of Getty Images.*

In those five seasons, Beck averaged 36 saves. After he recorded 37 saves in 1997, second in the league, he became a free agent and signed a four-year contract with the Cubs worth $17 million. Can you blame him?

When he left, Beck was the Giants' all-time saves leader with 199. To replace Beck, the Giants obtained Nen in a trade with the Florida Marlins and he proceeded to move past Beck as the Giants all-time saves leader.

Beck had his best year with the Cubs in 1998, saving 51 games, again second in the National League. A year later, he was traded to the Red Sox, and he wound up his career with the Padres, finishing up with 286 saves, more than Wilhelm had in 21 years and more than Stu Miller and Marv Grissom combined.

Statistical Summaries

All statistics are from player's Giants career only.

PITCHING

G = Games

W = Games won

L = Games lost

PCT = Winning percentage

SHO = Shutouts

SO = Strikeouts

ERA = Earned run average

Relief Pitcher	Years	G	W	L	PCT	SHO	SO	ERA
Hoyt Wilhelm *First pitcher to appear in 1,000 career games*	1952–56	319	42	25	.627	41	385	2.98
Stu Miller *Pitched a 1–0 shutout for St. Louis Cardinals in his first major league start on August 12, 1952*	1957–62	307	47	44	.516	47	506	3.16

continued	Years	G	W	L	PCT	SHO	SO	ERA
Marv Grissom *Posted a 1.56 ERA in 43 games in 1956*	1946, 1953–57	285	31	25	.554	58	314	2.88
Robb Nen *Fanned 110 batters in 89 innings in 1999*	1998–2002	365	24	25	.490	206	453	2.43
Rod Beck *Rolaids NL Relief Man of the Year in 1994 with 28 saves in shortened season*	1991–97	416	21	28	.429	199	393	2.97

FIELDING

PO = Putouts

A = Assists

E = Errors

DP = Double plays

TC/G = Total chances divided by games played

FA = Fielding average

Relief Pitcher	PO	A	E	DP	TC/G	FA
Hoyt Wilhelm	35	124	4	5	0.5	.975
Stu Miller	57	169	6	18	0.8	.974
Marv Grissom	20	102	3	8	0.4	.976
Robb Nen	20	32	5	2	0.2	.912
Rod Beck	22	52	3	4	0.2	.961

TWELVE

Manager

In the first three decades of the 20th century, there was no more successful team in baseball, both on the field and at the box office, than the New York Giants, and no more popular and revered personality in New York than **John McGraw**, their fiery manager.

The Giants were John McGraw, and John McGraw was the Giants. His teams took on the properties of their manager—combative, contentious, confrontational, and arrogant.

McGraw managed the Giants for 29 full seasons and parts of two others, during which he won 10 pennants, finished in second place 10 times, and brought his team home in the first division (the top four in an eight-team league) six other times. He also managed the Baltimore Orioles for two and a half seasons, and his 33 years, 4,769 games managed, and 2,763 wins are all second to Connie Mack, who once said of his contemporary and frequent rival (they met in three World Series with Mack winning twice), "There has been only one manager and his name is John McGraw."

1. JOHN McGRAW

2. LEO DUROCHER

3. BILL TERRY

4. DUSTY BAKER

5. ROGER CRAIG

John Joseph McGraw was born in Truxton, New York, in 1873 and was an outstanding player for Baltimore and two other teams. The premier third baseman of his day, he batted .334 for 16 seasons, numbers good enough to warrant election to the Hall of Fame as a player. But his career as a manager overshadowed his playing.

McGraw was only 26, and at the height of his playing career, when he got his start as a manager. He was named player/manager of the Orioles in 1899. When the Orioles were disbanded in 1900, some 70 years before the advent of baseball free agency, McGraw was sold to St. Louis, but agreed to the move only after the reserve clause was removed from his contract. As a result,

John McGraw (left, with Connie Mack) was a Hall of Fame player as a third baseman, but his brilliant managing career far overshadowed his exploits on the field.

he was free to return as player/manager when Baltimore entered the American League in 1901.

His abrasive personality and fiery win-at-all-costs demeanor, which earned him the nickname "Mugsy" from teammates and opponents, caused McGraw to knock heads frequently with American League president Ban Johnson and prompted him to bolt from Baltimore during the 1902 season and take over as manager of the New York Giants of the National League with a four-year contract at $11,000 per year. It was a move that dramatically altered the course of baseball history.

A year after he left Baltimore, the Orioles were sold and relocated to New York. Had McGraw been in place as manager of the Orioles at the time, it's likely he would have come to New York as manager of the Highlanders (later renamed the Yankees). Oh, how the history of baseball would have been changed had that come about—McGraw managing Babe Ruth; McGraw's team being kicked out of the Polo Grounds instead of being the kicker-outer.

Instead, McGraw managed the team that would be the Highlanders/Yankees intercity rival and, eventually, their landlord in the Polo Grounds, until McGraw, envious that the Yankees were outdrawing the Giants in their own home, kicked the Yankees clear across the Harlem River to their new home, Yankee Stadium.

Largely through the managerial skill of McGraw, the Giants were top dog in New York through the first quarter of the 20th century, and the Yankees, Johnnies-come-lately to town, were merely second-class citizens—but not for much longer.

Always several steps ahead of his opponents when he was a player, McGraw had such a fierce desire to win that he would employ any tactic available, within or outside the rules. He was notorious for blocking, tripping, and obstructing base runners when the umpire was not watching. He baited umpires and opponents alike and was known for his frequent battles with the opposition, both figuratively and literally.

As a manager, he employed the same characteristics he displayed as a player. He was a ruthless and relentless irritant to opponents and a tyrant to his own players, which earned him the nickname "Little Napoleon." He was reviled by opposing managers and players, revered by Giants fans, and tolerated by his own players, because he won. He became the first National League manager to win four consecutive pennants, 1921–24.

His teams took on the personality of their manager, with an arrogance and swagger that seemed to say, "We're good and we know we're good."

McGraw had a gift for recognizing playing talent and the courage to make daring trades. He didn't hesitate to collect rejects from other teams, hard drinkers, neurotics, and troublemakers, and molded them into a winning team. On the field, he adopted a style of play similar to that of the Orioles teams for which he played. He favored the hit-and-run and stolen base, eschewed the sacrifice bunt, and predicted that batters' increased desire to hit the ball out of the park would be the game's ruination.

Ultimately, it was McGraw's arrogance that proved his undoing. When the Yankees, as tenants in the Polo Grounds, grew powerful with the addition of Babe Ruth and replaced the Giants as New York's dominant team, McGraw ordered their eviction from his ballpark. The Yankees moved across the river to the Bronx, built their own ballpark, and strengthened their dominance.

By 1932, after seven straight years without a championship, the Giants had slipped to the bottom of the National League. On June 3, with his team mired in sixth place, McGraw resigned as manager of the Giants and named first baseman Bill Terry as his successor. Less than two years later, on February 25, 1934, at the age of 60, John McGraw passed away in a New Rochelle, New York, hospital. He was elected to the Hall of Fame in 1937.

It would be impossible to find two men more different than Mel Ott and **Leo Durocher,** my first two major league managers.

Where Ott was soft-spoken, Durocher was loudmouthed and boisterous.

Where Ott was gentle, Durocher was pugnacious.

Where Ott was laid back, Durocher was fiery, combative, and ruthless.

With all that in mind, you can imagine the reaction from players and fans when, on July 16, 1948, the Giants suddenly announced that Ott had been let go as manager and, simultaneously, announced that Durocher was replacing him.

We were shocked, to say the least. We were confused. And we took the news with mixed emotions. Even the writers who covered our team were upset because they all liked Ott so much, and they didn't like it when that guy Durocher came in to replace their beloved Mel Ott.

Most of the Giants players were sad for Ott, a man we all admired and respected for his decency and warm-heartedness. At the same time, most of us were outraged that Durocher, a man we had come to despise, was the one

Leo Durocher, shown arguing a call, was as fiery and cantankerous as they come. But the man knew his baseball, and he certainly knew how to win.

replacing him. One day Durocher was the manager of the Brooklyn Dodgers and our number one enemy, and the next day he was our manager. We didn't know what to think. But most of us didn't like it.

On the other hand, although we didn't like him, most of us respected Durocher for his knowledge of the game and for his desire. He was a winner, and we were certain he would make us better. At the same time, we were apprehensive about what it would be like playing for him.

Durocher had been a "good field, no hit" shortstop in the 1930s with the famed St. Louis Cardinals Gashouse Gang of Pepper Martin, Joe Medwick, Frank Frisch, and Ripper Collins, a rambunctious band of hard-nosed players that, no doubt, helped form Leo's personality. After the 1937 season, the Dodgers sent four players to St. Louis in exchange for Durocher. The Dodgers were a mediocre team at the time, and they believed Durocher's fire was what they needed to help them become a contender. There also were reports that Durocher was brought to Brooklyn to be the Dodgers' manager-in-waiting.

When they finished seventh under Burleigh Grimes in 1938—their sixth straight year in the second division—Grimes was fired and Durocher was named player/manager. The transformation in the Dodgers was immediate. In Leo's first year as manager, they improved by 15 games and finished third. Two years later, he led Brooklyn to its first pennant in 21 years.

In seven of Durocher's first eight years as manager, the Dodgers finished no lower than third seven times, the one exception being 1944 when their best players were off serving in the military during World War II. Durocher had imposed his indomitable will on his players, and with his penchant for bench-jockeying and umpire-baiting that earned him the nickname "the Lip," he was a huge hero in Brooklyn, a symbol of that borough's feistiness.

Revered in Brooklyn, Durocher was reviled in other National League cities, especially across the East River in Manhattan. It was Durocher, more than anybody else, who fostered the bad blood between the Dodgers and Giants.

But in the ninth year of Durocher's Brooklyn reign, trouble erupted. He was suspended from baseball for a year by Commissioner Happy Chandler for allegedly consorting with known gamblers and was replaced by Burt Shotton, a veteran, old-time player, scout, coach, and minor league manager, who, like Connie Mack of the Philadelphia Athletics, managed the team in civilian clothes.

To some he was unscrupulous, unsavory, boisterous, combative, profane, a supreme egotist, a rogue, and a scoundrel.

To others he was charming, engaging, debonair, dapper, a leader of men, and a winner.

To one and all he was Leo Durocher, "Leo the Lip," a relentless umpire-baiter and bench jockey, and among the most colorful and controversial figures in the annals of baseball. He wore the latest fashions, frequented the most popular establishments, associated with the most important people, and turned mediocre teams into champions.

He sought the company of the beautiful people, married an actress, Laraine Day, and buddied up with Frank Sinatra, Don Rickles, Danny Kaye, George Raft, and Jack Benny.

And he uttered some of the most outrageous, self-serving, and inflammatory statements:

"Nice guys finish last."

"As long as I've got a chance to beat you, I'm going to take it."

"Baseball is like church. Many attend, few understand."

"Buy a steak for a player on another club after the game, but don't even speak to him on the field. Get out there and beat them to death."

"I don't care if the guy (Jackie Robinson) is yellow or black, or if he has stripes like a goddamn zebra. I'm the manager of this team and I say he plays."

"Give me some scratching, diving, hungry ballplayers who come to kill you."

"God watches over drunks and third basemen."

"Nobody ever won a pennant without a star shortstop."

"Show me a good loser and I'll show you an idiot."

"How you play the game is for college ball. When you're playing for money, winning is the only thing that matters."

"In order to become a big league manager you have to be in the right place at the right time. That's rule number one."

"If you don't win, you're going to be fired. If you do win, you've only put off the day you're going to be fired."

"I believe in rules. Sure I do. If there weren't any rules, how could you break them?"

"I come to win."

"I made a game effort to argue, but two things were against me, umpires and the rules."

"I never questioned the integrity of an umpire. Their eyesight, yes."

"If I was playing third base and my mother was rounding third with the run that was going to beat us, I'd trip her. Oh, I'd pick her up and brush her off and say, 'Sorry, mom,' but nobody beats me."

"Some guys are admired for coming to play, as the saying goes. I prefer those who come to kill."

"What are we out at the park for except to win?"

"Win any way you can as long as you can get away with it."

"You argue with the umpire because there is nothing else you can do about it."

"You don't save a pitcher for tomorrow. Tomorrow it may rain."

"It was Brooklyn against the world. They were not only complete fanatics, but they knew baseball like the fans in no other city. It was exciting to play there. It was a treat. I walked into that crummy, flyblown park as Brooklyn manager for nine years, and every time I entered, my pulse quickened and my spirits soared."

"Luck? If the roof fell in and Dizzy Dean was sitting in the middle of the room, everybody else would be buried and a gumdrop would fall in his mouth."

"Joe Medwick never lost a debate in his life, mostly because he didn't bother. He was a one-man rampage."

"There is a thin line between genius and insanity, and in Larry MacPhail's case it was sometimes so thin you could see him going back and forth."

The presumption was that Shotton was merely keeping the manager's seat warm until Durocher returned from his suspension, but when the Dodgers won the 1947 pennant under Shotton, there was a groundswell of sentiment to keep him as manager and dump Durocher.

Nevertheless, Durocher resumed the Dodgers' managerial reins in 1948, but the team floundered at the start, and by the middle of July, the Dodgers had a losing record and were in fifth place. Coincidentally, the

Giants also had a losing record and were just percentage points ahead of the Dodgers.

Having decided to remove Ott as manager, Giants owner Horace Stoneham asked Dodgers president Branch Rickey for permission to talk with Shotton about the vacancy. To Stoneham's surprise, Rickey said the Dodgers were about to bring Shotton back as their manager, but they would give Stoneham permission to talk with Durocher about their manager's job.

It was quite a shock when Durocher took over our team. Leo never suffered from an inferiority complex and in his first meeting with us, he stood up in front of the team and said, "Forget all that stuff you've been reading about and hearing about; all that matters now is Giants…Giants…" and he swiped his hand across the name "Giants" on the front of his uniform.

Under Durocher, we had a winning record in the second half of 1948, but we still finished fifth and Durocher wasn't satisfied. He told Stoneham "this isn't my kind of team," and he worked hard to convince Stoneham to make changes, the kind of changes Stoneham was reluctant to make because the team that set the home-run record in 1947 brought the fans out to the Polo Grounds in droves. Despite finishing fourth, the Giants set a franchise attendance record with more than 1.6 million fans, an increase of almost 400,000 over the previous year.

Durocher kept hammering away at Stoneham, saying he wanted "my kind of player," and telling him that in the long run, a championship team was the best way to assure that attendance would soar. Durocher's "kind of player" was one who could run, play defense, and had the will to win. Toward that end, he convinced Stoneham to release Johnny Mize, unload Walker Cooper on Cincinnati, and trade fan favorites Sid Gordon, Buddy Kerr, and Willard Marshall to Boston for Alvin Dark and Eddie Stanky. It was that trade that was the making of our championship team in 1951.

"I need that protection at second base," Durocher explained. "I can't get the pitchers I want and I've got to have that double play to hold down the scoring against us."

It didn't take long for me to put my feelings about Durocher behind me and to appreciate that he wanted to win and to win at all costs. He'd get on players from the other team, battle with umpires, steal signs, and cheat to win if he had to. I don't know if he was stealing the signs himself or if somebody was stealing them and relaying them to him, but Leo would stand in the third-base coach's box and if he yelled, "Sock it," that meant a fastball was coming.

We all laughed about it and I didn't like it very much. I never liked cheating any way and I especially didn't like getting the signs. A lot of hitters don't like getting the signs. Suppose it was the wrong sign, you're liable to get killed.

You could see Durocher's influence on us almost immediately. He was aggressive. He put pressure on the other team. If Durocher was out there, the other team had to be on its toes. If, for example, Dark got a base hit to the outfield, you'd better get that ball into second base quickly because Dark was going to be tearing around first base looking to go to second. That was the kind of aggressive baseball Durocher preached.

There were times Durocher would get to be a pain because he never kept quiet. You heard so much of him. You could put up with it when you were winning, but when things weren't going so well, it would get on your nerves. If it was the middle of the season and we started getting a little slow sliding into second base, he'd call a meeting and get all over us.

"Hey, look you guys," he'd say. "You better not wait until the end of the season and then come to me and wonder why you're not getting more money. Now's the time to earn it, so get out there and hustle."

Only one time did he ever get on me. It was in Cincinnati and I was up all night, sick from something. I came to the park with hardly any sleep and I didn't get to a ball Leo thought I should have caught and he jumped all over me. That was the only time he ever singled me out for rebuke.

Of course, it all came together for us under Durocher in 1951. A lot about that final playoff game is all a blur. What I do remember is rounding third base and Leo trying to grab me and I pushed him away so I would be sure to step on third base.

The film, which I've seen a few times, shows that as soon as the ball went into the stands, Leo had removed his hat and was waving it and he was jumping around. And then the next thing you see is Stanky running out to the coach's box and wrestling Durocher to the ground.

That kept Durocher from getting to me, and he even said later, "I couldn't get Stanky off my back."

One thing about playing for Durocher, in addition to his ability to get the most out of his players and mold them into winners, there was always something going on around him. Leo had the ability to talk and he liked to wear fancy clothes and hang out with celebrities. He was married to the actress

Laraine Day, a beautiful and charming woman, and his friends were show-business people, not baseball people.

In New York, he fancied himself a Broadway personality, hanging out in places like Toots Shor's or Sardi's with actors and musicians. In Los Angeles, he liked to be seen in the company of movie stars.

There were always celebrities hanging around the team, especially in spring training. One spring, he had a party and invited all the players. At the party were Ava Gardner, Danny Kaye, Jack Benny, and Groucho Marx. It was fun meeting those stars. With Leo around, those were exciting days, on the field and off.

On June 3, 1932, with his team floundering in last place and in failing health, John McGraw abdicated his throne and resigned as manager of the New York Giants, the team he had piloted for almost 31 years. It was an announcement so stunning that it knocked off the lead sports pages the tremendous batting accomplishment of the Yankees' Lou Gehrig, who had hit four home runs in Philadelphia on that same day.

Equally stunning was McGraw's choice of first baseman **Bill Terry** as his successor.

The two men had never been particularly close, although Terry had been McGraw's best player for the past five seasons. Most observers thought if McGraw stepped down, the job would go to one of his two former short-stops, Davey Bancroft or Travis Jackson. Once Terry was named, Bancroft, then a coach, submitted his resignation and Jackson asked to be traded (he was accommodated the following year).

In 1932, Terry took over an aging, rag-tag team and brought it home in sixth place but managed to win the pennant in 1933.

Not deluded by his surprising success, Terry knew the Giants were in need of rebuilding and he set about to begin that enormous task. But first he would write his name into the book of quotations with one of the most well-remembered, off-the-cuff remarks in baseball lore.

It came at the baseball meetings in the winter of 1934 in a conversation with baseball writer Roscoe McGowen of *The New York Times*. Asked about the many deals that had been completed during the meetings, Terry noted that the Giants' intercity rivals, the Brooklyn Dodgers, had made no trades.

"Is Brooklyn still in the league?" Terry wondered.

The comment found its way into print and Dodgers officials took it as a slur on their team's playing ability, which it was not, and turned it into their rallying cry for the 1934 season.

The Dodgers were a well-beaten sixth in the National League, but the Giants and Cardinals were tied for first place when Brooklyn and New York met for the final two games of the season. In St. Louis, the Cardinals won both their games against Cincinnati. Meanwhile, at New York's Polo Grounds, the

Bill Terry poses with an unidentified man during the 1934 season, when he inadvertently fired up a non-contending Brooklyn Dodgers ballclub with a comment in the off-season and paid for it on the final day of the regular season.

Dodgers swept the last two games against the Giants and knocked them out of the pennant. Terry's remark had come back to bite him, and his critics, of which there were many, said it was the arrogance of his remark that had cost the Giants the flag.

After finishing in third place in 1935, Terry rebuilt the Giants around Mel Ott, Travis Jackson, and Carl Hubbell and won consecutive pennants in 1936 and 1937. Although he never was a favorite of writers (he was often curt and discourteous with them and refused to give them his home telephone number), Terry was a hero to Giants fans.

He managed the team for four more seasons, finishing in the second division three times, and resigned after a fifth place finish in 1941, but stayed on as general manager.

Many believe Terry's unwillingness to cooperate with writers cost him early election to the Hall of Fame. He was finally enshrined in 1954, 18 years after he had played his last game.

To his credit, Terry was gracious in his acceptance speech in Cooperstown. He didn't exhibit any bitterness or publicly condemn the writers for the delay.

Hard to believe that **Dusty Baker** managed the Giants longer than any other manager except John McGraw, 10 years, from 1993 through 2002. He also won more games (840) than any other Giants manager except McGraw.

Bill Terry also was the manager of the Giants for 10 seasons, but he took over for McGraw in June of his first year, 1932, so he didn't have 10 complete seasons as manager. Baker did.

The interesting thing about Dusty is that while he had an outstanding 19-year major league career as a player with four teams—a .278 lifetime batting average, 242 home runs, 1,013 RBIs, and two All-Star selections—he was a Giant only one season, 1984, when he signed as a free agent. By then he was 35 years old and on the downside of his career, but he batted .292 in 100 games.

After two more seasons with the Oakland Athletics, Baker retired after the 1986 season. A year later, he returned to the Giants as a coach under Roger Craig and stayed a Giants coach for five seasons. When Craig left after the '92 season, the Giants took a big gamble by naming Baker manager.

I say it was a gamble because the only managerial experience Dusty had was in the Arizona Fall League in 1992.

Dusty Baker was a three-time Manager of the Year award winner in his 10 seasons at the Giants' helm.

Baker's first year as a manager was nothing short of sensational. He led the Giants to 103 victories, their highest win total in 21 years and the most wins by a rookie manager in National League history. Unfortunately for him, the Braves won 104 games and beat the Giants out of first place in the NL West. Nevertheless, Baker was voted National League Manager of the Year, the first of three times he won the award (he also was chosen in 1997 and 2000).

After three losing seasons, Baker and the Giants bounced back to finish first or second in their division in each of the next six years, reaching the World Series in 2002.

Despite his success, a rift developed between Baker and Giants owner Peter Magowan. Dusty felt unappreciated. He thought he wasn't given enough credit by Magowan for the job he had done—eight times finishing first or second, five times winning at least 90 games, three times making the post-season, and three times winning the Manager of the Year award.

It's conceivable Baker and Magowan would have eventually worked out their differences and Dusty would have continued on as manager of the Giants. But he felt it was time to make a change, to look for a new challenge, and in 2003 he signed on as manager of the Chicago Cubs.

There's an old saying, "Those that can, do; those that cannot, teach."

That saying applies to **Roger Craig**.

I don't want to say that Craig couldn't pitch. He spent 12 years as a pitcher in the major leagues and anybody who does that has to be pretty good. But in those 12 seasons, he won 74 games and lost 98, and in his case, he was a better teacher than he was a pitcher.

Craig is widely acknowledged as the godfather of the split-finger fastball, the modern variation of the old forkball, a pitch held between the index and

Roger Craig is considered the inventor of the split-fingered fastball, and Jack Morris and Mike Scott were two of his most effective disciples. *Photo courtesy of Bernstein Associates/ Getty Images.*

middle fingers. Ideally, it's thrown with the same motion and arm speed as a fastball, but it kind of slips out of the grip and dives down just as it reaches the batter. When it's effective, the pitch slips under the hitter's bat beneath the strike zone.

Apparently, Craig didn't use the pitch when he played, but developed it after his career was over and taught it to other pitchers. As pitching coach of the Detroit Tigers under Sparky Anderson, he taught the split-finger to Jack Morris, who used it to win many of his 254 games.

In 1985, Craig taught the pitch to Mike Scott of the Houston Astros, who had been a struggling 5–11 the previous year. With the split-finger, Scott won 18 games in '85 and again in '86, when he also led the league in earned-run average, innings pitched, and strikeouts and was voted winner of the Cy Young Award.

Before he earned the reputation as a pitching guru, Craig had had a brief but unsuccessful two-year stint as manager of the San Diego Padres in 1978 and '79. After he earned acclaim for his work with pitchers, Craig, although he had never played or coached for them, was hired by the Giants to take over as manager in place of Jim Davenport in the final weeks of the 1985 season, when the Giants lost 100 games and finished last in the NL West.

The following year, the Giants won 83 games under Craig and moved up to third place, and the year after that they won the NL West championship. Two years later, the Giants again won the NL West under Craig, beat the Cubs in the Championship Series, but lost to Oakland in the World Series that was interrupted by an earthquake.

The next three years, the Giants showed a steady decline and Craig was let go after the 1992 season and replaced by Dusty Baker.

Statistical Summaries

All statistics are for manager's Giants career only.

MANAGING

G = Games managed
W = Games won
L = Games lost
PCT = Winning percentage
P = Pennants
WS = World Series victories

Manager	Years	G	W	L	PCT	P	WS
John McGraw *Came out of retirement to manage NL in first All-Star Game in 1933*	1902–32	4,424	2,583	1,790	.591	10	3
Leo Durocher *Twice managed two teams in one season (1948 Dodgers and Giants, 1972 Cubs and Astros)*	1948–55	1,163	637	523	.549	2	1

continued	Years	G	W	L	PCT	P	WS
Bill Terry *Placed no lower than third place each of his first six full seasons (1933–38)*	1932–41	1,496	823	661	.555	3	1
Dusty Baker *Led Giants to three of their top-five victory seasons in San Francisco (1997, 2000, 2002)*	1993–2002	1,556	840	715	.540	1	0
Roger Craig *Finished first in 1987 just two years after team lost 100 games*	1985–92	1,152	586	566	.509	1	0

Index

Entries in italics denote references to photo captions.

ROGER BRESNAHAN • WALKER COOPER • SHANTY H○
WILLIE MCCOVEY • ORLANDO CEPEDA • JOHNNY MI
LARRY DOYLE • BURGESS WHITEHEAD • EDDIE STAN
DICK BARTELL • BUDDY KERR • FREDDIE LINDSTROM
RAY HART • BARRY BONDS • MONTE IRVIN • JOE MC
CHILI DAVIS • HANK LEIBER • BENNY KAUFF • GARRY
DON MUELLER • FELIPE ALOU • CHRISTY MATHEWSC
LARRY JANSEN • CARL HUBBELL • RUBE MARQUARD •
WILHELM • STU MILLER • MARV GRISSOM • ROBB NE
TERRY • DUSTY BAKER • ROGER CRAIG • ROGER BR
LOMBARDI • WES WESTRUM • BILL TERRY • WILLIE M
LOCKMAN • FRANKIE FRISCH • JEFF KENT • LARRY I
JACKSON • ALVIN DARK • DAVE BANCROFT • DICK B
WILLIAMS • SID GORDON • JIM DAVENPORT • JIM RAY
IRISH MEUSEL • KEVIN MITCHELL • WILLIE MAYS •
MADDOX • MEL OTT • BOBBY BONDS • ROSS YOUNGS
• JUAN MARICHAL • GAYLORD PERRY • SAL MAGLIE •
ART NEHF • JOHNNY ANTONELLI • BILLY PIERCE • HO
• ROD BECK • JOHN MCGRAW • LEO DUROCHER •